Proud to Be Chickasaw

ELDERS OF THE CHICKASAW NATION ⊛ VOLUME II

Proud to Be Chickasaw

ELDERS OF THE CHICKASAW NATION ⚘ VOLUME II

by Mike & Martha Larsen
and Jeannie Barbour

CHICKASAW PRESS

ISBN: 978-1-935684-01-5

Chickasaw Press
The Chickasaw Nation
P.O. Box 1548
Ada, Oklahoma 74820

Book and Cover Design: Skip McKinstry

Proud to Be Chickasaw

Foreword by Governor Bill Anoatubby vii

Preface x

Acknowledgements xv

Daisy Blackbird—*Our Oldest Citizen* 3

Bea Barrick—*The Milkyway Girl* 8

Beaulah Shavney—*She Served Her Country* 16

Thelma Lucile "Chincie" Ross—*Code Talkers* 24

Colbert Hackler—*The Fiddle Player* 33

Eugene "Gene" Thompson—*I'm So Proud To Be Chickasaw* 40

Glenda Galvan—*Patron Saint of Children* 47

Irene Digby—*Cherished One* 54

John Atkins—*Infant Boy Atkins* 62

Juanita J. Keel Tate—*She Knew My Father* 69

Katherine McGuire—*Memories of Her Dad* 77

Kennedy Brown—*Indispensable* 85

Lenora Hobbs—*Elegant* 92

Lorena Wooley—*Chilocco*.. 97

Luther John—*Keeper of History* 103

Mabel Edna Smith—*She Whispered*... 110

Marvin Mitchell—*Proud of His Sons*.. 117

Philip Agnew—*Sober Indian*... 124

Robert Woolley—*The Cattleman* 131

The Milligan Siblings: Geneva Ducote, Raymond Milligan, Ruby McKinney—
Days of Hoover Hogs 139

Weldon Fulsom—*How Turtle Got Its Shell*... 147

Zane Browning—*Too Tall*.. 154

Bernard Courtney—*Water Bread and Water Gravy* 159

Mike Larsen, Artist... 169

Martha Larsen, Writer.. 171

Mike Larsen, *Curriculum Vitae*.. 173

Foreword by Governor Bill Anoatubby

It is true that our elders speak us into existence. Long before I existed, my elders were here. They imagined me in their thoughts and dreams, and heard what their elders said about generations to come, and finally those dreams came true and I was born. The elders are like eagles. Their close vision may be no better than yours or mine, but their long vision is keener, more precise. They have the long view, and they love us. Mike Larsen knew this, or at least sensed this very strongly, when he proposed a bold experiment in 2004.

"What do you think about a portrait series of living Chickasaw elders?" he asked. From that initial inspiration, the first collection of 24 elders paintings, and the book, *They Know Who They Are* (Chickasaw Press 2008), were born. The reception for the first series and for the book was so positive that a second series was commissioned. This book presents Mike's second series of masterful portraits of Chickasaw elders.

While the rest of the world praises the amazing work of Mike Larsen, Chickasaw citizens are truly blessed to receive these valuable works into our national collection. As in the first series, as Mike sketched, during their visits to the elders, Martha Larsen listened to each of the elders' stories, and later recorded her impressions in writing. The visual and written portraits thus produced are stunning to me, and I trust that any reader of this book will be moved.

I am deeply grateful to Mike and Martha for their great work, and to others who deserve credit as well. As with the first volume, the best resources of the Chickasaw Nation came to bear to bring the project, and now the book, to fruition. Once again, the professional artists and designers of Lona Barrick's team in the division of arts and humanities have assisted the Larsens in bringing this dream to reality.

It is my prayer that the elders who are revered in this book will be with us for many more years. We depend so much on the legacy of their lifetimes of work, and upon their blessings and deep wisdom, to face the battles of each day with courage and bravery.

Eagles sail over our forests, rivers and lakes, mountains and prairies. They are vigilant in the protection of their young, establishing their nests at altitudes no predator can reach. They provide for their young and teach them to look and listen before they teach them to fly. In the same ways, our elders are vigilant for us. They are confident in what they have taught us, and certain that we will not depart from their teachings when we are old. Our elders reach back to their elders and give us wings to fly, as they sail like eagles above us, close to the sky. We sense that vigilance and wisdom in these portraits. It is in their wisdom, songs and stories that we, and future generations, will continue to thrive.

Governor Bill Anoatubby

Proud to Be Chickasaw

The statement, "I am very proud to be Chickasaw," was expressed in twenty-three emotional and expressive ways by the elders portrayed in this magnificent series of paintings by internationally acclaimed Chickasaw artist Mike Larsen.

With a strong voice echoing fierce pride, in quietly humble tones, or with lilting humor, each remarkable person also expressed to Mike senses of firm resolve and purpose, and connection to the shared history and legacy of the Chickasaw Nation and its people.

The journey that produced *Proud to Be Chickasaw* began in the summer of 2004, when Mike approached Governor Bill Anoatubby with his desire and idea to honor our elders for their status as wisdom-keepers, and as the foundation of the tribe. Mike, assisted by his wife, Martha, conducted interviews, took photographs, and made sketches that produced the first exhibit in the Chickasaw elders series, *They Know Who They Are*, which opened to acclaim in November 2007, and became a book published by the Chickasaw Press less than a year later.

The first series was, in Mike's words, "a life changer." Not only did he begin to more fully understand his identity as a Chickasaw and feel a stronger connection to it, his work, he told me, became "better, richer." Mike also recognized the impact the paintings of our treasured elders had on all who saw them and read the stories behind them.

In 2008, Mike asked to continue the tribute. Governor Anoatubby fully supported his request, and Mike, again accompanied by his wife, Martha, began the next steps in the journey. With the assistance of the Nation's arts and humanities division, they began.

Mike and Martha were again welcomed into the homes of our Chickasaw elders. The elders' family members often were part of the interview process. Many generations offered helpful examples of the teachings, stories and values their elder loved ones had shared.

As in the first series, the elders in *Proud to Be Chickasaw* had unique stories and shared experiences. Most survived the difficult years of the 1930s, when a nickel could buy not just a Milky Way® candy bar, but a bit of happiness for a little girl. Many told exciting stories, and spoke proudly of their experiences and sacrifices during World War II, like one of the first women to serve in the Women's Auxiliary Army Corps, and another who worked with the Navajo Code Talkers. They spoke with pride and humility about being part of what has come to be known as "the Greatest Generation." Many recalled attending church and Chickasaw community meetings under brush arbors, wherein the future of the Nation was discussed, debated, nurtured and developed, and of being part of the "new" beginning of the Chickasaw Nation's government as it is today.

Most elders in the first series lived in Oklahoma, several within the boundaries of the Chickasaw Nation, and some still on their families' original allotments. While many in the second series also lived in Oklahoma and on old family land—like one who still operated the family's Centennial ranch east of Ada—several lived elsewhere. Those elders, although far from the "center" of Chickasaw activity, maintained loyalty, connection and identity with their tribe.

The amazing exhibit I *am Very Proud to be Chickasaw* opened in October 2009 at the Gaylord-Pickens Oklahoma Heritage Association Museum in Oklahoma City, Oklahoma. A driving rainstorm could not keep most of the elders and their families from attending the crowded, standing-room-only event, which also attracted state and tribal dignitaries.

The second in the portrait series presents an impressive, beautifully expressed masterpiece. The portraits reveal diplomats, culture bearers, historians, musicians, artists, teachers, ranchers or homemakers, and are tributes to the individuals portrayed and to their pride in cultural heritage, family, country and beliefs.

These works of art are more than just paintings on canvas, or prints on pages. Each represents a life lived with conviction, a thirst for knowledge, and a willingness to work hard and help others in need. Each depicts an individual who holds a steady gaze, who is hopeful and compassionate, and who expresses appreciation for life and the joy it brings.

All paintings in the series also can be seen at the Chickasaw Cultural Center in Sulphur, Oklahoma.

Mike Larsen has given to us an amazing gift, not only of beautiful artwork, but of a greater connection as a tribal nation, as a family and as a people. It is difficult to find the right words, or enough of them, to thank Mike and his lovely wife, Martha, for their commitment to honoring our treasured elders.

Much thanks is owed to Governor Bill Anoatubby, without whom the series would not have been realized. Governor Anoatubby's appreciation for our elders and the lessons they teach us, together with his desire to share that knowledge with others, have made it possible. On a personal note, I thank Governor Anoatubby for his commitment to the arts and his understanding of their integral role in the cultural and historical legacies of the Chickasaw Nation and its people.

Lieutenant Governor Jefferson Keel also has given continuous support. Sincere appreciation goes to the many family members who graciously helped to arrange visits and interviews. Gratitude also goes to the many Chickasaw Nation division administrators for their quick and constant assistance.

Much thanks also goes to the staff of the division of arts and humanities, especially Joanna Underwood, Rachel Westmoreland and Marcus Milligan, who assisted with interviews. Angela Owen and Kevin Scrivner of the Chickasaw Press aided with several interviews and skillfully managed transcriptions. Thanks also to Jeannie Barbour for her sensitive touch with writing, and, Glenda Galvan, Mary Hartley, Pat Woods and Karen Cook for their invaluable help.

The heartfelt thanks owed to the elders who opened their doors and shared their stories cannot be overstated. Their humility, strength and perseverance, and their appreciation for life, for family and for their rich Chickasaw heritage are gifts to us all.

Lona A. Barrick
2010

Acknowledgements

I would like to acknowledge the incredible gift given to Martha and myself by the elders who allowed us to visit their personal histories. Each visit helped me understand my own family and provided us with brothers and sisters we will always have.

Thank you also to Lona Barrick, Joanna Underwood, Mary Hartley, and Jeannie Barbour. I want to especially thank Governor Anoatubby for his understanding and for making it possible for us to portray all these wonderful people.

Mike Larsen

2010

Proud to Be Chickasaw

ELDERS OF THE CHICKASAW NATION ⊛ VOLUME II

Daisy Blackbird | *Our Oldest Citizen*

Daisy Blackbird was born January 18, 1903, near Tupelo, Indian Territory (I.T.). Her parents were Arthur E. and Elizabeth Colley Hawley. Elizabeth, who was born in 1883, spoke Chickasaw exclusively until she started school. Elizabeth, who was one-half Chickasaw, and four other members of the Hawley family, including Daisy, were given 160 acres of land each in Coal County after the Dawes Commission enrolled them as Chickasaw citizens following the turn of the century. The second oldest of ten siblings, Daisy took care of her younger brothers and sisters in their first home on her mother's allotment. "My mother married at a young age. I was one of the oldest, so I took care of the younger ones. There were seven girls and three boys," Daisy recalls.

Daisy's parents owed their marriage to the Oklahoma Land Run of 1889. Arthur's father, Edwin Hawley, participated in the run and settled near Britton, I.T. Eventually, Edwin moved to a farm near Byrd's Prairie, I.T., where his son Arthur went to work for William M. Colley and his full-blood Chickasaw wife, Lucy. Arthur soon met and married Elizabeth, the Colleys' daughter.

The Hawleys were farmers, and like other Chickasaw families of the time, they worked long, hard days. The family owned cattle and kept a large garden and a peach orchard. Everyone had daily responsibilities in the house and in the fields. Social life revolved around the changes of the seasons. School programs, church gatherings, and trips into town were special occasions spent with family and friends.

Daisy's family moved into the town of Tupelo, Oklahoma, when she was nine years old. The Hawley children attended school there. "In the small town of Tupelo, my father was very important. He was on the school board," Daisy explains. "When we moved to town, we lived in a big, two-story home. It was a beautiful place."

Daisy graduated from high school to attend Kansas State Teacher's College in Pittsburg, Kansas. After college, she returned to Oklahoma to teach in one-room schoolhouses in Tupelo and Coalgate. "In those days, we had all age groups in one room. I spent a lot of time with the fourth-grade children," she remembers fondly. Eventually, she took a job in Oklahoma City as a payroll clerk for the state Supreme Court. It was there she met her late husband, Oklahoma Chief Justice William Henry "Bill" Blackbird. "I was a payroll clerk for the Supreme Court. He was an elected judge from Muskogee. He had just bought a new car—a Buick. He asked me if I wanted to take a ride. I ended up married and lost my job. But it was worth it,"

Daisy remembers, gleefully. "We both couldn't work at the Supreme Court."

Daisy clearly recalls the hardships of the Great Depression. "I remember the Depression well. I can't forget the bad things, like people not having new clothes very often, like some people not having enough food or enough medical care. There wasn't enough money to hold things together. But, I remember the good things, too, like people coming over to visit on the porch at night without our wondering what they wanted. People would stop and help a stranger fix a flat on the road. Like people just pulling together. The Great Depression, as bad as it was, had a little good in it. I'm glad I was here then and I am glad I'm here now."

Quilting, crocheting and painting were activities Daisy enjoyed for many years. Today, she shares a home with Wanda Montgomery, her 87-year-old sister, in Oklahoma City. Daisy's own floral and landscape paintings decorate its walls. When asked what was most important to her about being Chickasaw, she remarked simply, "Well, it just comes natural." Daisy is one of the last surviving original Dawes enrollees. As such, Oklahoma Governor Brad Henry honored her in ceremonies at the State Capitol in May 2008. At 107 years of age, Daisy Blackbird is the oldest living Chickasaw.

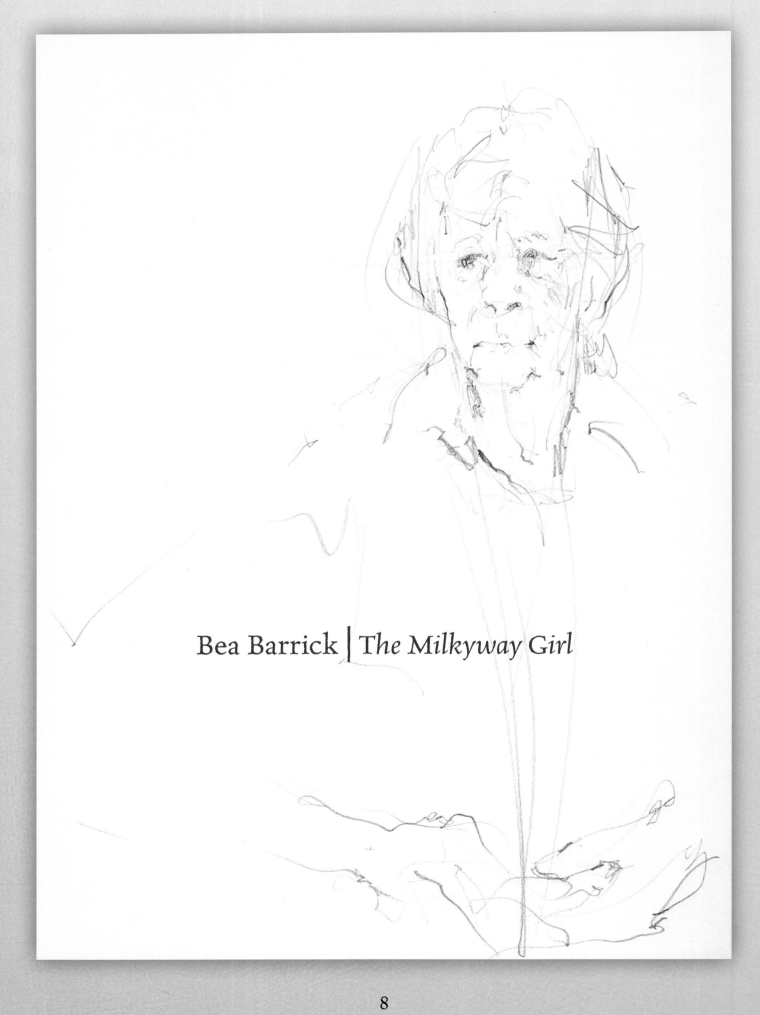

Bea Barrick | The Milkyway Girl

Leona Beatrice "Bea" Barrick belongs to a large, warm, tightly knit, loving family. She was born October 19, 1923, to Nathaniel and Rosa Antoinette "Nettie" Brown in Berwyn, Oklahoma. Nettie had borne twelve children before she died during childbirth at age 38 in 1927. She suffered pneumonia complicated by a heart condition, and the child was stillborn. Bea never knew if the infant was a boy or girl, but remembers her mother and sibling were buried together.

Bea's father Nathaniel, a Chickasaw citizen, suffered from Huntington's disease most of his adult life. A progressive neuro-degenerative genetic disorder, Huntington's destroys muscle coordination and causes memory loss and speech impairment.

"My grandpa (Charles A. Brown) was married to Josephine Kemp. She was a white woman. She had Huntington's disease, and it is hereditary. That's where my Dad got it. Most of his siblings had it, and most of mine did, too," Bea explains.

Charles' father was Joshua Brown, who was married to a Choctaw woman named Nancy Curtis. Charles and Joshua were Chickasaw. The family's allotment was near the Arbuckle Mountains in Davis, Oklahoma.

Bea's family worked hard to make ends meet during the Great Depression. "We used to go places and pick cotton for people. We'd just go around wherever people needed work done," she says. Despite his uneven health, Bea's father fought to provide for his family, and vowed to his children, "The family stays together."

Bea recalls an instance from when she was five years old that illustrated his commitment. "We were on our way to Texas to live with my oldest sister. She was already married when my mother died. We were in an old truck and my brother was driving. My Dad was up front with him. The rest of us were in the back with our belongings. The old truck died going up a hill. It rolled backward and overturned. I guess God was looking out for us. None of us were hurt very badly. A man and woman, strangers to us, lived nearby. They took us to their house and helped us. They had no children, so they wanted to adopt my younger sister and me. With my Dad's condition, I guess they thought he could not take care of us," Bea recalls. However, "Dad always believed in keeping the family together. That's why we were going to my sister's in Texas," Bea says.

Bea's family also moved for a short time to Ardmore, Oklahoma. "I remember when we lived there, my dad taking me and my youngest sister. We would walk into town to go to the barber shop to get our hair cut."

The Brown family moved often, living in Berwyn, Ardmore, Empire, and Duncan, Oklahoma, as well as parts of Texas and California. Bea started school in Ardmore, and continued after she moved to Texas to live with her older sister, Viola Brown Strickland.

Bea attended school until the ninth grade. "I loved to read. I read everything I could get my hands on. You can imagine if you have to work all the time at home. It was kind of a vacation time," Bea recalls. "I made good grades. One year we couldn't go to school, 'cause we didn't have any shoes … things like that."

She also enjoyed lunch period. "A lot of times we had free lunches, and sometimes we didn't get to have lunch. You could buy things real cheap then. There was a little store by the school, kids would go over and get stuff to eat. I had a dime. I guess I got it from one of my brothers or something, for my lunch. This store had chili buns, and of course, they had candy. I would go over there and get me a chili bun and a Milky Way® bar every time I had the money. It got to where every time

I went there, the store clerk would say, 'Here comes that Milkyway girl!'"

Bea also worked outside the home waiting tables, cleaning houses, ironing, and washing laundry. She was sixteen when she married Willis Benton Barrick in July 1940, after her brother, Joe Nathan Brown, introduced them. Willis worked near Duncan for the Civilian Conservation Corps, a public work relief program. She recalls him as an excellent mechanic and an excellent dancer. They would have six children together.

Eventually Bea and Willis moved their family to Ada, Oklahoma, where Bea stayed home to take care of the children. "I didn't want anyone else taking care of my kids. Sometimes I would do babysitting to raise extra money." After her youngest child started school, Bea took a job at the school's cafeteria. "I just kind of felt like I was at loose ends," she says.

For years, Bea belonged to a bowling league in Ada. "The best game I ever bowled was a 249. We'd go to state tournament and go to the nationals. I really liked it. We went to Las Vegas, Connecticut, Reno, Louisiana, and Baton Rouge. Last time we went to bowl, we went to Fort Lauderdale. I was still bowling in a league when my husband passed away in 2003," Bea recounts. "Now I play cards and go to church, of course."

Bea has thirteen grandchildren, thirteen great-grandchildren and four great-great-grandchildren. Nathaniel Brown's philosophy of taking care of family lives on in Bea Barrick, and she has passed it on to the next generations of the Barrick family: "If you can't count on family, who can you count on? If somebody needs a place to stay, come on. You don't turn your family away."

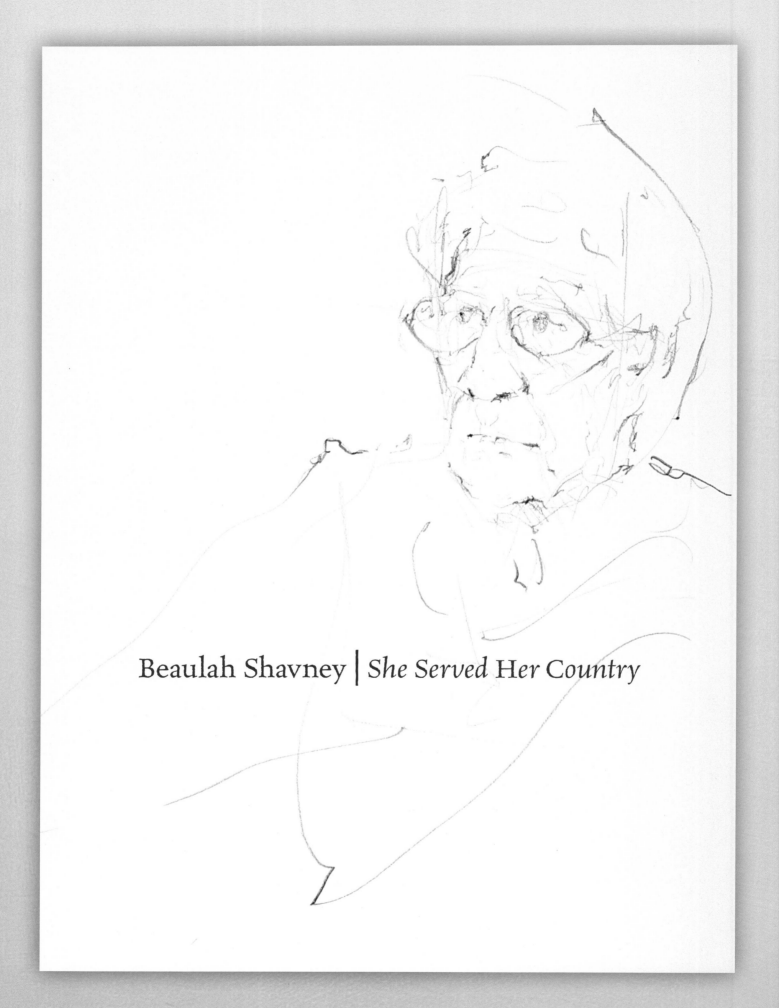

Beaulah Shavney | *She Served Her Country*

Beaulah Shavney was born April 2, 1922, in Marlow, Oklahoma, to Orbie Lee and Sylvia Pope. Her mother was a full-blood Chickasaw/Choctaw; her father was a non-Indian.

Beaulah grew up helping on her family's farm during the Great Depression. "We milked the cow and raised everything we had. We were poor like most everyone else at the time." Beaulah remembers eating lots of biscuits, gravy and pinto beans, and, "I loved my mother's grape dumplings!" Although there was plenty of work to do, she also spent time at the creek behind the family home. "We used to go wade up and down that creek. We loved to do that. When we could, we would visit other family members who lived close enough. There was never any money to travel great distances." One of her cousins was Pearl Carter Scott, the famous aviatrix.

Beaulah's mother worked in a laundry and liked to crochet. "That was one thing—she was talented. She could make anything. I used to go to these shows, and I would find something small I thought was real pretty, and I would buy one and take it home, and she would make it. I never could crochet."

Sylvia's sister Nancy married Joe Bethune, a hawker in a medicine show. Medicine shows were popular from the late 1800s until as late as 1972. They were commonly associated with "miracle elixirs" (some called them "snake oil"), which were touted to have a variety of purposes, like curing ailments, smoothing wrinkles, removing stains and prolonging life. Beaulah recalls, "When I was a kid, every once in a while they would take me. We'd go around and he'd (Joe) get out and stand up there and holler their medicine. That was fun!"

Beaulah's grandparents were Josiah and Emily Gibson. Beaulah remembers Emily going out into the woods and returning with plants and other natural materials to treat people who came to her for help.

Education was important to Beaulah's parents. She attended Marlow schools until the ninth grade, when she was sent to Chilocco Indian School, a federally run boarding school near the Kansas-Oklahoma border that taught academic and vocational skills to Indian students. Beaulah remembers it fondly, saying, "I was really very happy there, after getting over being lonesome for a few weeks. But then, you would form bonds with other students. We became a big family. I took arts and crafts and other classes. We had chairs that we strung yarn on. We would sit and weave yarn together to make a belt. I wish I could remember how to do that."

After graduating from Chilocco in 1940, Beaulah joined her parents, who had moved to Phoenix, Arizona. She worked at a variety of jobs for a year to save money to attend Gregg Business School, where she learned office skills. She graduated in record time and immediately found a job at the Phoenix Indian Hospital as a secretary for one of the doctors.

She held the job for a year, then decided to join the military. "They started recruiting women. I was there, and I thought it was something I would like to do. I went down and applied. They wouldn't take me. I was too skinny. They said, 'You go home and come back in a month.' I guess they thought they were rid of me. I ate bananas and straight cream for a month. I went back. I was about a quarter-pound short of being heavy enough. But, they took me." Beaulah enlisted in May 1943. She

didn't know she was blazing a trail for women in the armed services as a charter member of the Women's Auxiliary Army Corp (WAAC). Later she was transferred into the Army as part of the Women's Army Corp (WAC).

Beaulah was stationed at Fort Knox, Kentucky, where she served on the clerical staff for the commander of the Armored School for two and a half years. While in the service, she met and married native New Yorker Richard Hugo Shavney.

"We met on a blind date. We went to midnight Mass," Beaulah explains. "My mother was not very happy about me marrying a Catholic. She was a strong Baptist. My dad was not happy about it, either. When they met him, they liked him." Richard, also in the service, was sent to the Philippines six months after the couple married. Beaulah left the service in December 1945 and Richard followed soon after.

The Shavneys had three children together. Richard was a machine operator, and Beaulah worked in several places, including an insurance company and a bank. She also became interested in quilting. "I would get one quilt finished and would immediately start another. I guess I have 10 or 11 quilts. I made one for each of my 10 grandchildren," says Beaulah.

Beaulah and Richard lived in New York before they moved to Sand Springs, Oklahoma, to be close to her parents. Richard died in 1968. Beaulah continued to live in Sand Springs until 2002, when she moved to Ada, Oklahoma. Today, she lives quietly among family and friends. She enjoys puzzles and attends the annual Chilocco reunions. "I go back, and it is just like meeting brothers and sisters," she concludes. "I notice, as the years go by, there are fewer of us. Now, I don't know if people just don't come or they are fading out. I know I've lost a lot of my friends."

Beaulah is proud to be Chickasaw. "Chickasaw is just something you want to be. We are always striving to accomplish something. We are always looking to find what is out there."

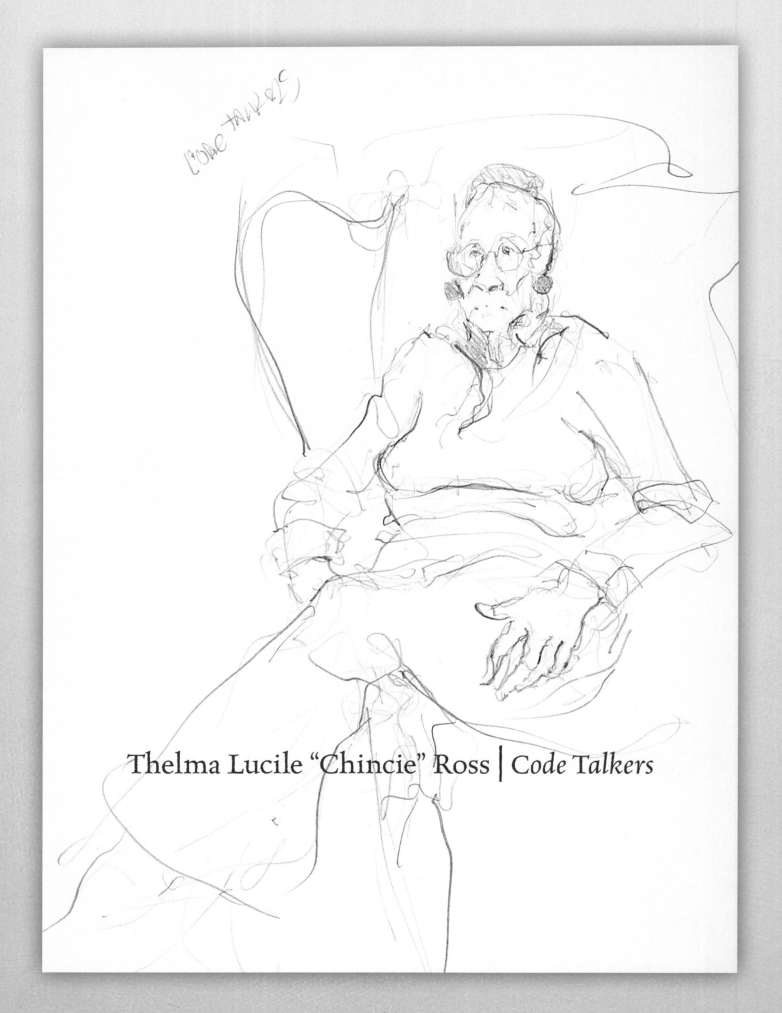

Thelma Lucile "Chincie" Ross │ *Code Talkers*

Thelma Lucile "Chincie" Ross was born September 9, 1917, near Tuttle, Oklahoma, to Turner and Susan Bell Downing Cochran. "My mother had six children—three boys and three girls. My baby sister died at 18 months of age, of spinal meningitis. She was the prettiest thing there ever was," Chincie recalls.

The name "Chincie" was given to her by her father. "He had always said that 'Chincie' was an Indian word for 'beautiful flower,'" Chincie says, fondly. Turner's parents were Elick (Cherokee) and Arnica Tarnatubby-Wolf Cochran (Chickasaw).

When he was younger, Turner drove cattle and performed in a Wild West Show in Montana. "Papa was quite the little rounder," Chincie says. "Cute as a bug. He was bowlegged from years spent in the saddle. He also delivered mail by horseback across the country—like the Pony Express. I still have his saddlebag."

In 1904, Turner went to work on John David Downing's ranch near Verden, Oklahoma. There he met and fell in love with the rancher's daughter, Susan Bell Downing, named after the infamous "Bandit Queen" Belle Starr—a distant relative by marriage. "My mother was a smart lady. She was educated at

Chilocco Indian School and at Haskell Institute. She thought she would be working someplace for the government—a secretary in an office. That was quite the thing back then. She had taken her Civil Service test and passed. My grandmother 'Katzenjammer' (her real name was Margaret Leonard Downing) didn't want my mother to leave," Chincie explains. "She intercepted the report and didn't let her know about it. So Mom married Papa instead. They got married in Anadarko in 1907."

The Cochrans established a ranch on their allotment lands near a town called Silver City. In 1925, Turner replaced the frame home with a cement-block house that had no plumbing or electricity. "Papa always said, 'You can't go to the can and eat under the same roof,'" Chincie laughs. "My parents did not have indoor plumbing until 1958. That is when my husband and I put it in for them."

Chincie recalls the hardships of the Great Depression. "I remember the dust storms. Mom would have to wet sheets for us so we could breathe. We slept out in the yard. The dust covered everything," she recalls.

The Cochran children began their education in Silver City,

where their father sat on the school board. The schools later were made part of Tuttle's district. Chincie excelled in athletics and scholastically, well enough to earn a scholarship to Central State University. Unfortunately, a freak stomach injury she suffered while playing basketball interfered. "Someone threw a chair and hit me. They took me to the hospital and the doctor said I would get over it. But I never did," Chincie says. Soon Chincie was back in the hospital to have her appendix removed. A long convalescence cost her the scholarship. Chincie decided to attend her mother's alma mater, Haskell Institute, to study business.

Chincie recalls that wasn't easy, either. "When I got up there, I had to stay in the hospital because of the appendix problem. I would walk to class, clear across campus."

After graduation, Chincie went to Concho, Oklahoma, to work with the Cheyenne-Arapaho tribe. Later she traveled to Window Rock, Arizona, to work with the Navajo at the Fort Defiance hospital facility. After World War II began, she was asked to help process young Navajos recruited by the Marines to serve as the famed Code Talkers.

"After that, I was loaned to the Poston War Relocation Center," Chincie recounts. "They had three camps there in 1942."

Poston, on the Colorado River Indian Reservation in Arizona, was the largest of ten internment centers that housed American citizens of Japanese descent after the attack on Pearl Harbor in 1941. Internees called its three camps Roastin, Toastin and Dustin. "Some of them (internees) would get off the train, and that hot air would hit them and they'd pass out. They were not used to the desert climate," Chincie says.

It was then that Chincie met her future husband, Richard William Ross. "I had started working at the Pima Indian Agency at Sacaton (Arizona). Dick was in the Army and stationed at the POW camp at Florence," Chincie recounts. "They housed German and Italian POWs. We got to know one another at a place called Desert Beach." With Chincie's parent's blessing, the couple married in 1947. They would stay a short time in Ohio, then move to Oklahoma to establish a home in Tuttle.

Chincie's high school injury, however, kept them from having children of their own. "After the war we tried and tried to have children. I had one miscarriage after another. We decided to adopt. I tried the government program first. Then we found a child through the state—Susie," Chincie says. The Rosses adopted Susan Eleanor, a Choctaw child, in 1949. They adopted a second child, Allen William, of Cherokee descent, in 1955. "I wouldn't adopt any children unless they were Indian, and they had to be (of) the Five Tribes."

Dick passed away in 2005. Chincie still lives in the home they shared in Tuttle, and is a beloved member of the community. In 2009, Tuttle High School honored Chincie during their 100th year celebration. She served as parade marshal during homecoming. "They dedicated the school yearbook to me. I rode in a horse-drawn wagon!" she exclaims. "It was a very special day. The folks here are so good to me."

Chincie is committed to her family. Along with her two children, she has seven grandchildren and sixteen great-grandchildren. "Family is everything. Papa taught us that you don't get up in the morning without thanking the good Lord for the beautiful day and the ones you love."

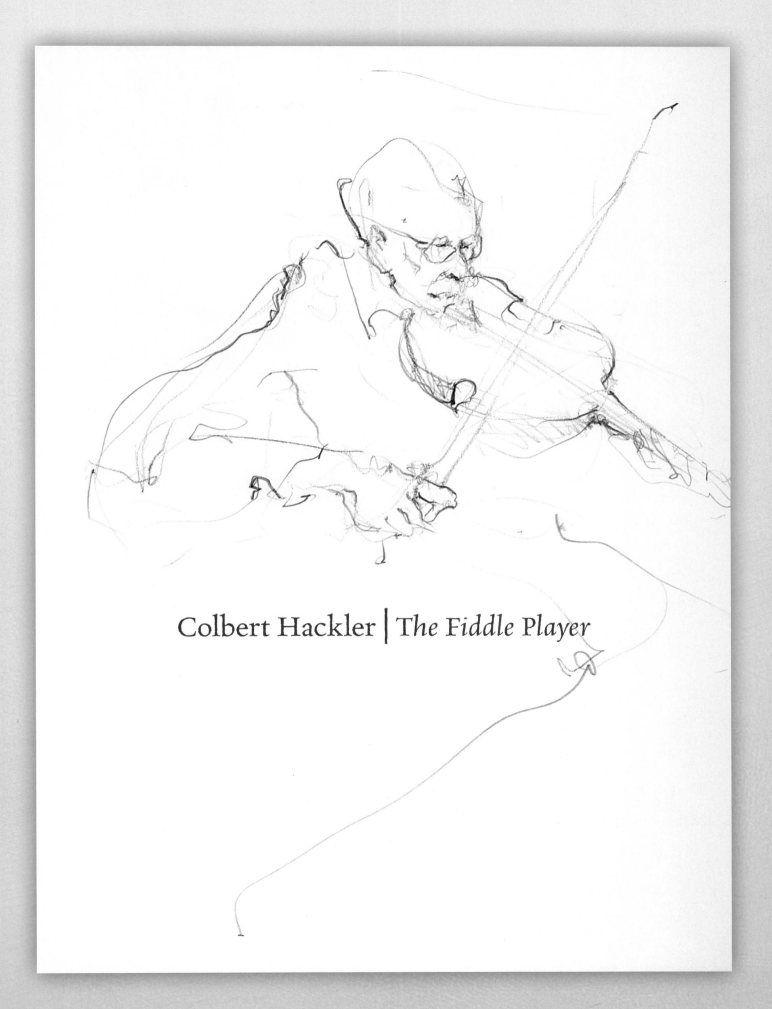

Colbert Hackler | *The Fiddle Player*

Colbert Hackler was born January 13, 1918, in Mannsville, Oklahoma. Colbert, his brother Harold, and their parents lived a quiet life. Colbert's mother and father noted his interest in music at an early age, and bought him a violin for Christmas when he was eight.

Soon after, the family moved to Ravia, Oklahoma. No one there could teach violin to young Colbert, so his parents sent him to the local piano teacher. The teacher and the boy shared notes and thoughts, and Colbert learned to play mostly by ear. Eager for more, he listened every day to WBAP's western swing radio show from across the Red River in Dallas, Texas, featuring Bob Wills and the Light Crust Doughboys. He learned a great deal by mimicking the fiddle playing of the "King of Western Swing."

Eventually, the family moved more than fifty miles west to Ringling, Oklahoma. While there, Colbert's father, a lumber-yard manager, found a violin teacher in Ardmore who would give lessons to his son. After high school, the talented young musician entered Oklahoma City University, where he earned a bachelor of fine arts degree in music in 1943. Colbert soon accepted a job with Elk City public schools, and committed 17 years of his life to developing the music program there.

His quiet, gentle demeanor was perfect for teaching elements of music to young people.

Colbert was a member of the local Methodist church, where he and his wife, Mary Jean, were active in the music program. His civic commitment to Elk City was so well noted that in 1952 city leaders proclaimed a "Colbert Hackler Day." By the time Colbert left Elk City, he had helped to establish a high school band, a junior high band, an elementary school band, a beginner's band, a high school mixed chorus, two glee clubs, and a junior high mixed chorus.

In 1960, Colbert left Elk City to work on his doctorate in music at the University of Oklahoma. There, he taught both vocal and instrumental music at the University Laboratory School. When it was closed in 1971, he was moved to the main campus of the School of Music. There, he served as advisor for students seeking certification as instrumental music teachers in the public school system. Again the talents of many students were developed over the years through his gentle, unassuming teaching style. His gifts were shared with others, too—Colbert also would put on performances at retirement homes in the Norman area.

Sadly, Colbert lost his beloved wife to cancer in 1982. He retired for a time, but soon felt the need again to be involved in music and teaching. Upon his return, he became interested in the Suzuki method of music instruction, developed by Japanese violinist Shin'ichi Suzuki in the mid-twentieth century. The method seeks to develop skill through music immersion and support. Students are encouraged to take small steps while learning, and are immersed in an environment rich with a variety of art forms and means of self-expression. Its goal is to build the student's character through a nurturing atmosphere. Colbert adopted the method for his pupils, which included his two daughters, Maryanne Tullius and Sally Rice. He also has five grandchildren and four great-grandchildren.

For more than sixty years, Colbert Hackler has brought the joy of music to the lives of thousands. His goal was not so much to create a classical "Julliard" kind of student, but to develop one who enjoys making music. Shin'ichi Suzuki once said, "If a child hears fine music from the day of his birth, and learns to play it himself, he develops sensitivity, discipline, and endurance. He gets a beautiful heart." In his later years, Colbert Hackler has applied the Suzuki method to his own life, and has helped create a better world because of it.

Gene Thompson
I'M SO PROUD TO BE Chickasaw

Eugene "Gene" Thompson | I'm So Proud To Be Chickasaw

Eugene Glen "Gene" Thompson was born October 14, 1937, to Thomas Benjamin Thompson Jr. and his wife, Thelma Flovel Dabney Thompson, in Oklahoma City. Thomas Jr. upholstered furniture for a living, and Thelma was a housewife.

Gene and his sister, Taloah, grew up in a warm and loving home. Some of Gene's fondest childhood memories are of family gatherings. "I think of the family reunions we used to have. We used to have a pot of pashofa and we would tell stories," said Gene.

Gene's grandparents were Thomas Benjamin and Alberta "Birdie" Thompson. Thomas Sr. was full-blood Chickasaw; Birdie was of German descent. After losing both his parents, Thomas Sr. grew up in an orphanage. At fourteen, he went to stay at the Chickasaw White House in Emet, Oklahoma, with his aunt Nellie—the first wife of Douglas Johnston, future governor of the Chickasaw Nation. He later entered into a successful partnership with Johnston in the mercantile business.

Thomas Sr. was an original Dawes Commission enrollee whose allotment land was near Butcher Pen, Oklahoma. "My grand-daddy, because of the time they lived in, wanted his children to learn English. He knew they needed to survive in the white man's world. He would tell stories in Chickasaw to his kids. That's how Te Ata learned her trade. She listened to him tell stories in both Chickasaw and English," Gene explains.

He thereby introduces us to his aunt, the great Te Ata Thompson Fisher, Thomas Sr.'s daughter. The world-renowned Native American actress and storyteller, whose career spanned eight decades, gave performances before President Franklin D. Roosevelt and the king and queen of Great Britain, among others.

"When she would come and visit us, it was kind of like festival time. She had done all these wonderful things as a famous entertainer. She never had children of her own, so her nieces and nephews were kind of like her kids. She mothered us in a lot of ways. She told us about our Chickasaw history and gave us our Indian names—it was something we were all proud of," Gene remembers fondly.

Gene attended schools in Oklahoma City. "I have always said, 'I was a poor kid in a rich man's school.' Consequently, most of my youth was spent working hard at various jobs. I also joined the National Guard when I was sixteen. I was in the 45th Division—the Thunderbirds," he says. As a high school student, Gene excelled in photography and was given a scholarship to attend Cameron University in Lawton, Oklahoma. It was there that he met his future wife, Vivian. Together they had two children, Howard Thomas and Melissa Anne Baldwin. He also developed an interest in entomology, the study of insects. Gene's academic success attracted the attention of the U.S. Department of Agriculture (USDA), which selected the young man as one of 13 students to participate in their entomology program, studying at Oklahoma State University. Later the USDA secured a job for him at the University of Nebraska.

The Army and the Air Force took notice, and offered officer's commissions to Gene in 1960. He chose the Army, and went to Fort Sam Houston to serve as a medical entomologist. Over the next twenty-nine years, Gene traveled the world, and became the first entomologist to be assigned to the office of the Secretary of Defense. He retired as a full colonel in 1983, and moved to Austin, Texas.

Over the next four years, Gene was a pest management and sanitation consultant to food and pharmaceutical industries. He then took a job running HIV/AIDS field studies for the Texas Department of Health before retiring again in 1999.

From an early age, Gene was taught the responsibilities of leading a good life—an Indian life. Gene declares, "My grandfather stressed to me when I was growing up that, the Indian way was to put your values in the Creator, in your country, and in your 'Indian-ness.' All Indians were important to him. You were to always serve your community. He gave more away at his stores than he sold. He would see a person in need and make sure they got what was essential to make their life better."

Gene's father was given Thomas Benjamin Thompson Sr.'s allotment land, 340 acres of which are now under Lake Texoma.

"When my dad was getting old, he said, 'What do you want?' I said, 'I don't want a thing. You go and spend every penny and enjoy life. But I don't want anybody to have that Indian land.' Just a couple of years ago, my sister and I gave the last bit of what was left of the allotment to our kids," Gene says.

Today, Gene is active in the Austin area as an ambassador for the Chickasaw Nation and an advocate for Native American culture and history. He is asked to give talks at civic organizations, seminaries and schools about Chickasaw culture, religious beliefs and practices. He helped to organize the

Chickasaw Community Council in Austin as a 501(c)(3) nonprofit organization whose swelling membership meets ten months out of each year. Its many accomplishments include the creation of a library of Native American books available to the community.

"I am so proud to be Chickasaw," says Gene. "I like what I am doing and am interested in seeing our culture spread."

Glenda Galvan | *Patron Saint of Children*

orn July 30, 1954, at Olney, Oklahoma, to Thomas
Cecil and Leona Catherine Reed Ayakatubby, Glenda
Galvan has spent most of her adult life in service
to others. She was raised in the Mennonite faith, which
emphasizes such service. "I was always told that the first thing
placed in my hands after I was born was a Bible," Glenda says.
"Religious faith has always been an important part of my life."

She remembers her childhood, with siblings Loretta, Charla,
Sharon and Gary, as happy. The Ayakatubby family moved to
Kansas the year after she was born.

"I was raised on a dairy farm. My father milked seven days
a week, twice a day. By the time I was a sophomore in high
school, Dad went into the oilfield," Glenda says. "He'd come
in at 3:30 in the morning. He would be milking by 4 a.m. His
day didn't stop until the sun went down, because there was so
much to do."

Leona Ayakatubby was a stay-at-home mom. "When we got off
the bus, we would help Mom," Glenda recalls. "We would do
laundry, clean or whatever. I was always the cook. My mom
loved to teach me to cook. Mom always had cookies, cake or

pies ready and baked for us when we came home from school. We never had to wonder what we were going to eat or if we were going to eat. After the work was done, we were free to roam the country. We would ride our bikes down the section roads and come home when it was time to eat dinner."

Glenda has fond memories of her grandparents, as well. John Cecil and Rosie Lee Ayakatubby-Taylor, her father's parents, spoke the Chickasaw language—Glenda says she was a teenager before she knew Rosie could speak English—and owned a corn grist and sawmill. "My paternal grandpa John Cecil had a shop. He always kept the Chocolate Soldier pop for us because he knew that was our favorite pop. He was very attentive to us kids. My grandmother (Rosie) was the best cook. They lived on their allotment. Their house is still there. My grandpa built it when he came back from the navy in 1948, and I was born in one of the bedrooms," Glenda adds. Her grandfather's allotment is still within the family. Glenda's sister Loretta Taylor lives there today.

The Chickasaw language was important to the Ayakatubby-Taylor family. Thomas Cecil taught his children words and phrases. "I'm still trying to pick up more than I ever have before, and I'm teaching my granddaughter. It was important to us because that is the first thing we all did when we got together. Everyone likes to know and speak their own language," Glenda says. Glenda's maternal grandparents, Thomas Jefferson (T.J.) and Lola Virginia Wright Reed, spoke Chickasaw as well.

Chickasaw stories were a special matter. "My granny (Rosie) would like to tell stories. I would get paper and start taking notes, and she would get up and leave. She thought if you can't remember it, then you do not need it. I learned real fast I had to either retain the stories by memory or just forget it. She told the leaning pole story—the one with the great white dog. It is the story of how Chickasaws came to be in the homelands."

And Rosie's stories offered strength when times weren't so happy. "When I was a senior in high school, my parents decided to get a divorce. I was very upset by this. Seeing how sad I was, she told me the story called 'The First Divorce.' That story comforted me and helped me through a tough time. It made me a stronger person."

Glenda has been asked to share her stories with children and adults across the United States and abroad over the years. She has passed many of them on to an understudy, Lorie Robins.

Unlike many Chickasaw families, the Ayakatubbys knew where their ancestors' homelands were. "At least once or twice a year, we take my little granddaughter to Bear Creek in the homelands so she can dip her little feet in the water. It is located just across the Alabama state line (from northeastern Mississippi) on the Natchez Trace. We want her to know where she comes from," Glenda says.

Glenda has worked for the Chickasaw Nation for the past twenty-six years, and is the Manager Curator for historic sites in the Division of History and Culture. She has done extensive research on Indian Territory, Oklahoma statehood, and Chickasaw families. She has served as a translator at Carl Albert Indian Health Facility in the languages of the Chickasaw and Kickapoo tribes.

Glenda's family was known for generosity. "My dad, Grandpa, and his dad were all successful. Their success allowed them to help others in a time of need," she remembers. In that regard, one of her most remarkable achievements is her commitment to the Chickasaw Nation Foster Care program. She has fostered numerous Indian children over the years.

"My mother was a big influence when it came to my ideas about raising and nurturing children," Glenda explains. "She was always there for us. I have loved every child that came into my home. I am proud of them all and the progress they are making. My greatest joy is helping others. There is a great deal of satisfaction in being able to meet and serve fellow Chickasaws. It is like we are a huge family."

Irene Digby | *Cherished One*

The "Roaring Twenties" was an era of great optimism and prosperity, the beginning of modern America. Henry Ford built the Model T. Radio found its way into virtually every home. The first "talkie" motion picture, *The Jazz Singer*, came to theaters. Charles Lindbergh flew across the Atlantic in the *Spirit of St. Louis*. And Irene Digby was born. Her birth on November 12, 1921, to Joe and Serena Fulsom Pettigrew truly was a cherished event for the family.

"I was born between Davis and Sulphur (Oklahoma) in a little place called Fairview," Irene says. She had a sister, Loreene, and two half-sisters, Caroline and Lucille. Later, the family moved to their allotment land in the Sunshine community in Murray County. "We lived in a little house. I think it had three rooms. I always called it the 'White House'. I had a happy childhood. We never fussed. I never heard my family fuss. Our family was close to one another. Most of my relatives lived around there. They would come to visit often. Everyone was welcome," Irene remembers.

Church was the center of the Pettigrews' lives. Sandy Baptist Church was about two miles from Irene's home, and to get there, "We walked! We never griped. We enjoyed walking— everybody walked back then. My dad (Joe) was real faithful.

I think he was a deacon at Sandy. He never missed church. Momma would always cook her meals on Saturday. Never on Sunday! We didn't do anything on Sunday—the Sabbath day," Irene reminisces. "We would walk to church, carrying our food. We would stay all day until night, and then we would walk home.

"It was real interesting to go to church. My religious life started out there. I know I learned all the books in the Bible out there. Today it is different. I remember, as a child, we sang Choctaw hymns. Until this day, I still sing at my church. We have a little singing thing on Fifth Sundays. That is when I get to sing my Choctaw songs."

Like most Chickasaw families then, the Pettigrews were farmers. While Joe worked the fields, Serena held things together at home. "My mother and father, they were real, real Indian. They talked in our native tongue all the time. Mother couldn't speak English well. She was a great cook," Irene says. "We always had a big garden. Momma canned stuff. We also had chickens and eggs—everything we needed."

Traditional Chickasaw dishes were a special treat for the family. "Momma and daddy made pashofa in a big black pot. We always had Indian food. We liked roasted corn. It was a tradition in our

family," Irene remembers. "We would also make potato bread, blue bread, and fry bread."

By the time Irene was ten, the Great Depression gripped the country.

"Well, everybody was poor," she says. "But our family was rich, in a way. We always had plenty to eat because we raised a garden. I remember we couldn't get shoes. The government agents came and gave us a certificate to get shoes. One time, the agents came to school. They gave all the Indian girls material and 'brogans'—you know, shoes. They were the ugliest shoes. We were ashamed to wear them!" Irene exclaims. Through good times and bad, however, Joe and Serena made sure their children attended school, even if teachers discouraged use of the Chickasaw language.

Irene Pettigrew grew up, graduated from Davis High School, and went to work. She met B.F. "Dick" Digby, and married him. Private First Class Digby served in World War II, was decorated for valor, and spent time in Germany. Unfortunately, over time, his medals were lost. Irene has tender memories of the times she and Dick planted their own garden and raised beefsteak tomatoes. "He was a good *nahollo* man," she laughs.

Church was important to the couple. They moved their membership from Sandy Baptist to a church in Davis, and reared four children: Aaron Dean, Ronnie, Beverly, and Rhonda. "I also have eleven grandchildren and seventeen great-grandchildren. I have a wonderful family. I don't know what I would do without them. They look after me all the time, and they take good care of me. Every time one comes by to go somewhere, I jump in the car and go with them," she says, smiling broadly.

Today Irene attends Chickasaw Trail Baptist Church. She has lived in her same home for forty-seven years, and there lovingly tends her roses, which are of a variety without thorns. "A bush with thorns got hold of me once, and I didn't think I was going to get out of it alive," she jokes. Although Irene did not have anyone to speak Chickasaw with for many years, the language still is an important part of her life. She attends the Chickasaw Nation's language classes and is becoming familiar with her native tongue again. "I am glad to participate. My kids and grandkids can go, too," Irene enthuses. "My mother gave me the name of 'Ishki' Chokma'. It means 'Good Mother'. I am a proud fullblood Chickasaw." Irene is also the "cherished one" in her family—as she should be.

John Atkins | *Infant Boy Atkins*

John Atkins is a son of Jackson Atkins and Rosie J. Hayes Atkins, and one of their four children. John was born in the Talihina Indian hospital at 2:45 a.m. Thursday, July 25, 1941. He weighed seven pounds, ten ounces, and had very red skin. John knows these facts because his mother recorded in a diary every detail of the first seventeen months of his young life.

One matter was unclear, however: the baby's name. John's birth certificate reads simply, "Infant Boy Atkins." Depending on whom you talk to among family and friends, he is known as John, John Cohune, J.C., Jake, or Red. That wasn't all: "There was a preacher at church that called me Justin. Why he called me Justin, I do not know," John chuckles.

John's first photograph was taken at two months. He received his first pair of shoes at four months. When he was seven months old, he cut his first tooth, and Rosie hung a buckhorn around John's neck.

"I asked my mother about that. She had taken an antler and cut a piece of it off. She drilled a hole in the piece of antler and put a ribbon through it. Then she put it around my neck, like a necklace. She said that I would never have trouble with my teeth if

I wore the buckhorn as a child. It was believed that my teeth would grow straight and strong." But it wasn't for long. John later asked his mother what happened to the buckhorn necklace. "She said that she was giving me a bath one day. She laid it to the side of the washtub. A chicken came up and gobbled it down. That chicken walked around with a ribbon hanging out of its mouth. That is how I lost the buckhorn," laughs John.

John's family lived on his grandmother's allotment in Coal County. Her name was Mary Perry Atkins; his grandfather was Abner Atkins, and both were Chickasaw.

The Atkins family home did not have electricity for most of John's childhood. "We finally got electricity when I was in high school," John explains. "Up until that time, we used coal oil and lanterns. We would sit around in the evenings and listen to family stories." John's family told stories about shape shifters, little people and other Chickasaw beliefs. John's grandmother Mary spoke the Chickasaw language fluently. She also knew herbal remedies for minor ailments.

John was sent to Jones Academy in 1947. "I remember they (his parents) drove me up to Jones in a 1932 Chevrolet.

I remember watching the back of that car leaving. They put my stuff out and said goodbye, and that was it. I was six years old, standing there on the campus waving goodbye, feeling alone. I wasn't entirely alone, though. One of my brothers was already attending Jones," John says.

The young boy found Jones Academy to be a very large place in the beginning. Established four miles northeast of Hartshorne, Oklahoma, in 1891, the all-male school covered seven hundred and twenty acres, one hundred forty of them set aside for cultivation. Besides academics, the boys were trained in industrial arts, farming, dairy methods, engineering, blacksmithing, carpentry, and painting.

When John first arrived, he was considered a "Brownie" and assigned a bunk on the first floor of the dormitory with the younger children. The facility was heated by steam. "There were a lot of steam pipes in the place," John remembers. "There was a big shower room. They would run everyone in there at the same time to take a shower. For some reason, I always got shoved to the back, where the steam pipes were. I was always burning my back on the pipes."

John stayed at Jones for only a year, and went on to other schools in Stonewall and Tupelo, Oklahoma. "The Tupelo school would let out in the fall for cotton season. Our family used to travel around to pull cotton to earn money. My mother made the sacks. Mine was six feet long. We usually stayed in a barn. Sometimes there would be a house or a cabin on the property to stay in. I remember once pulling bolls in Clarita. I was standing out in a field with my dad. He said, 'You know, if you don't get an education, this is gonna be your life.' He only had a third-grade education and worked hard all his life as a farmer. My mother went to Bloomfield. I remembered what he said when I graduated from high school. I went to Haskell and learned a trade."

Haskell Institute, in Lawrence, Kansas, was established in 1884 by the federal government as an Indian industrial training school. John learned welding there.

After Haskell, John participated in the Urban Indian Relocation Program created by the federal government as part of assimilation policies in the 1950s. "I had originally decided to go to Chicago. I went to Dallas instead. My mother and father were living in Stonewall, Oklahoma, at the time. Dallas was closer," John explains. The program found John a job in construction. "I did

about a week of that and went back to the (government) office and told them, 'Find me another job! It's too hot out there!' It was summertime. With the helmet and everything you need to wear for welding out in the open spaces, things got pretty hot." Officials found John a job indoors, making ornamental iron furniture and fences.

Eventually, John earned enough to purchase a home in the Dallas area. He married three times and has had three children. Today, John lives in the same house with Darla, his wife of seven years.

Juanita J. Keel Tate | *She Knew My Father*

Juanita Jeanette Keel Tate was born September 10, 1910, to Guy, a farmer, and Lula Potts Keel, a schoolteacher, in Ardmore, Oklahoma. Juanita was one of twelve children— the rest were Overton, Willie, Cecil, Lewis, Irena, Lutie, Douglas, Franklin, Lucille, Minnie, and a stillborn boy. "When my dad came to see me after I was born, he picked me up, and mother said he held me and walked around the room. He said, 'She looks just like a little Foshi,'" Juanita says with glee. "Foshi" means "bird" in Chickasaw.

Juanita began public school in Hugo, and was a good student, no doubt influenced by her mother's commitment to education, which in turn pointed her in a direction that would become important. "My mother was educated at Bloomfield school. When she graduated, they placed her (to work) in a school that was later called Thompson Pickens School," Juanita relates. "It was a little two-room schoolhouse. When I interviewed one of my friends fifty years ago, she told me she was a former student in that school. She said they called it Thompson Pickens School because that was the name of the man who supplied the lumber to build it." Thompson Pickens was the son of Chickasaw leader Edmund Pickens, who led the tribe during removal to Indian Territory. Edmund Pickens also was Juanita's great-grandfather.

Like her mother, Juanita attended Bloomfield, but left after a semester because, "It was strictly for out-of-town Chickasaw girls. Bloomfield was located in Ardmore at the time. I was living in Ardmore, and couldn't stay."

In 1922, Juanita was enrolled in Chilocco Indian School, a federally funded institution that taught trades to Indian children. Chilocco was noted for its military-style discipline and curricula. "I want to tell you that was one of the best schools in existence in those days," Juanita insists. "The teachers were super and the classes well-rounded."

Tragedy intervened with the loss of her sister Lucille. "She graduated from (Chilocco) a year or two after I did. Instead of coming straight home, she chose to go to Pawnee and visit my married sister, who was living there. One of her Chilocco classmates, Blanche Rubidoux, was living there, too. They liked to go to the local pool and swim. One day, when they had just got out of the pool and were walking to the dressing room, a hit-and-run driver hit them. They lay there on the street before an older couple came along. Blanche died instantly. My sister lived a short time," Juanita recalls sadly. "After that, I couldn't get her off my mind, so I moved back to Ardmore to be with my mother."

Juanita enrolled in Ardmore Business School, and became adept at use of stenotype machines and in shorthand. Her remarkable skills were showcased in training sessions across the state. While in school, she met Ernest William Tate, an instructor and officer there. They were married, and Juanita continued to take courses at Southeastern Oklahoma State University in Durant, East Central University in Ada and the University of Oklahoma. Ernest took a job as a Carter County court clerk during the 1930s.

The country and Oklahoma suffered, however. "Times were rough during the Depression," Juanita admits. "The government handed out food at special places—especially down at the railroad tracks in various towns and cities. I got a job down there as a secretary to make note of everything that came in."

Later, Juanita's skills helped her find work at the district attorney's office in Ardmore. She worked for many years as a court reporter on the state and federal levels. Ernest and Juanita brought four children into the world—John, Roberta Anne, Gwendolyn and Charles Guy. Education remained important. She took extensions courses from O.U. and Southeastern Oklahoma State. She studied economics and history at E.C.U from 1959-60.

Ernest died in 1981, and Juanita since has been a devoted grandmother and great-grandmother. Family and history have been significant to her. "My father spoke Chickasaw fluently. My mother spoke some Chickasaw, but it was not her native language. My mother was one-quarter Chickasaw. My father's friends would come to the house. They would gather in the living room and speak Chickasaw to one another. My mother said I was always the one that would pull up a chair and sit down to listen," she says.

She spent more than 48 years researching and writing a book about Edmund Pickens, studying records in the Chickasaw homelands. The result was *Edmund Pickens (Okchantubby): First Elected Chickasaw Chief, His Life And Times*, published by the Chickasaw Press in 2008.

Juanita also has written articles about Chickasaw history and people. She has been a longtime member of the Chilocco National Alumni Association, and was inducted into the Chilocco Indian School Hall of Fame in 1987. She has been an active member of the Bloomfield-Carter Seminary Alumni Association, and was inducted into the Chickasaw Hall of Fame in 2008.

She considers establishment of the Keel family cemetery as one of her greatest accomplishments. Its cemetery association is a group of extended family members organized in the 1950s, and meets each year. The cemetery lies near where the Thompson Pickens School once stood, close to the family's original allotment near Lebanon, Oklahoma.

Asked what advice she would give to younger generations of Chickasaws, the centenarian says, "I would say, study history—the history of your tribe. It can be so fascinating, as you have children and grandchildren and all kinds of descendants. They are going to want to know about themselves and their family. Start a library. Be proud of your tribe. Do what you can do to help it continue. Visit the homelands—go back to land where you came from. Write the history of your family. It's all important."

Katherine McGuire | *Memories of Her Dad*

Katherine McGuire's close relationship with her father, Joseph "Joe" Cunningtubby, began at her birth January 5, 1919. She would be one of four children born to Joe, a full-blood Chickasaw, and his wife Sarah Malinda Davis.

Katherine lived most of her childhood in a modest house a mile outside Davis, Oklahoma, when there was little else but open field nearby. "Our house was on Baseline Highway. That is what they used to call it. It was a gravel road, and very few cars traveled on it. It was very exciting when they put asphalt down on that road for the very first time. It tickled us kids to death to get out there and run on that asphalt." Katherine recalls, still a little tickled.

Joe's mother was the nearest neighbor, a quarter-mile away. The land they lived on belonged to her as part of her Chickasaw allotment from the Dawes Commission, which had taken the liberty of changing the family name—to Cunningtubby from the original Kunauntubbee—without explanation.

"Her name was Sophie Cunningtubby. We called her Grandma. It seemed to me that she was tall. I always thought she looked so stately. She was a nice-looking lady. She could hardly speak

English at all. We dearly loved her," Katherine remembers fondly. "She died when I was eight years old, in an accident."

Joe worked hard to support the family. "He would come in from the fields where he had been working and pick me up and dance around while singing. I wasn't very big. He would say, 'Now, that makes me feel good! I am not near as tired as I was.' I looked forward to that every afternoon. I loved my daddy," Katherine reminisces.

The family lived on ten acres, five of which were used for farming, and Joe tended a large garden. "We usually had enough potatoes and everything to do us for winter. We never did go hungry." Eventually, Joe turned to selling gravel from two family-owned pits. Katherine notes everyone knew him to be honest in all his dealings.

As with many other Chickasaw families, church was a major part of Cunningtubby life. "Daddy sometimes had a car. Sometimes he didn't," she recalls. "I'll tell you what, though—we went (to church) Sunday mornings, Sunday nights, Wednesday night, and let it be revival, we went every night—rain, shine, cold or hot."

At one point, the family fell upon hard times. "Daddy took us (Katherine and her older sister Lula) up to Bloomfield. That year was kind of a bad year. He said, 'Girls, we may not have enough money to get your stuff for school.'" The girls were given a tour of the prominent Chickasaw boarding school for females. Joe asked Katherine if she thought she could live there. Katherine replied she would stay if Lula did, too. According to Katherine, Joe thought for a moment, and said, "Y'all get in the car; you're going home. I'm not going to leave you. We'll make it one way or the other."

"And we made it," Katherine emphasizes.

Joe spoke Chickasaw, as did many of Katherine's relatives, often as a first language. "But daddy said if we had to live in the white man's world, just go ahead and learn the English language. So he never did try to teach us Chickasaw. But he could speak it," she recalls proudly.

Katherine married Lewis Hensley at the height of the Great Depression, in 1937. Together they moved to Oklahoma City, where Lewis worked as a carpenter. Their first home was a room that rented for $3.75 a week. "We were poor as church mice,"

Katherine recalls. Their first child, daughter Melba, was born in 1938. "This lady let him (Lewis) have this little old house out in the country near Davis. It was an old house, you know, the kind that was made with boards—one put over the other. It had two rooms," Katherine says.

The economy grew worse, and Lewis could not find work. In desperation, he wrote to a senator about their plight. Soon a letter arrived announcing Lewis would be given a job earning $30 a month. "I got the letter out of the mailbox and started hollering and yelling. Lewis came running out from the barn; he didn't know what was wrong. I showed him that letter. I am telling you: We were down to our last dime," Katherine emphasizes.

In 1947, Katherine and Lewis moved to California, where their second child, another daughter named Marilyn, was born, and Katherine began working to help support the family. They would move back and forth between Oklahoma and California, with Katherine working at several jobs, and bringing two more children, Billy and Sandy, into the world. Their marriage lasted fifty-one years until Lewis passed in 1988. Sadly, Katherine had lost beloved father Joe in 1968. "I missed him so much after he was gone," she says. "I can't help it. If I am driving along and I see somebody like Daddy, an Indian man with a black rim (hat) with a dress coat and tie, I can't help but turn around and look." She also lost a daughter in 1996, her only son in 1999, and another daughter in 2002.

Katherine married Leroy "Bud" McGuire in 1995, and they were together four and a half years. Today, she lives and works for the Chickasaw Nation in Sulphur, Oklahoma. She has 17 grandchildren and more than 40 great-grandchildren. She stays active, playing cards, cooking and attending church.

Katherine advises younger Chickasaws "to hang in with their tribe. Be as good as you can be, so that nobody can say anything against our tribe. I am an Indian and proud of it. I am what I am and that's just it!"

Kennedy Brown | *Indispensable*

Chickasaw citizen Kennedy Wilson Brown was born in the family home north of Stonewall, Oklahoma, on May 19, 1939, to Lula and Adolphus Brown. Kennedy's family was prominent in the Indian Methodist Church, where his father served as a minister until he completed an education degree and began teaching in public schools. Kennedy's earliest and fondest memories are of times spent with his maternal grandmother, Elmina Leader, at her home located in the traditional Chickasaw community of Kullihoma. "Most everyone in the Kullihoma community spoke Chickasaw and held close ties. They helped one another—especially during the Depression years. No one went without. If someone needed help, the community provided it," Kennedy recalls.

His father's work frequently moved the family to different towns in Southeastern Oklahoma. As a result, the young boy learned to adjust to new situations and meet new people with ease.

In 1957, as a senior, Kennedy was transferred to Tupelo High School. His easygoing manner and love for people helped him to be elected as class president. "This was my first leadership role," he remembers. "It was a great experience for me. I learned many things." After graduation in 1958, Kennedy attended college at East Central University in Ada, Oklahoma, and took classes that would propel him into a career of social work.

Meanwhile, he landed a job at an Ada television station—KTEN, Channel 10. Kennedy agreed to play the irascible character "Cactus Jack" on a children's program called "The Bar Ten Roundup". In those days, local television was mostly live. "You had to think on your feet, and you never knew what to expect next." The program taught valuable lessons and entertained legions of children in the Ada area during the early 1960s.

Kennedy's desire to help people led him to a position as a counselor and field representative for the Neighborhood Youth Program in Ada, one of the Office of Economic Opportunities programs set up under President Lyndon Johnson's administration. His position required him to work with at-risk young people aged 14 to 21 who had not finished their high school educations. He helped many prepare for General Educational Development (GED) tests and develop job skills through training.

In 1974, Chickasaw Nation Governor Overton James saw an opportunity to capitalize on a newly established federal program for Indian people. Oklahoma Indian tribes were given an opportunity to receive grants under the Division of Indian and Native American Programs in the Department of Labor. Kennedy was interviewed and appointed to work with the program for the Chickasaw Nation. Thus began his 30-year odyssey of helping the Chickasaw people in a variety of capacities, always with a humble spirit of service.

From 1987-91, Kennedy served as Lieutenant Governor of the Chickasaw Nation. "It was a time of change for the Chickasaw Nation," Kennedy remembers. "With Bill Anoatubby as Governor, there were new ideas and the establishment of new policies that would lead us to a bigger, more sophisticated growth period for the tribe. It is amazing what has been accomplished for our people since that time."

Kennedy Brown has an impressive list of life accomplishments. He has served on the Chickasaw Historical Society board since its inception in 1994. He was appointed to the first Chickasaw Tax Commission. He currently serves on the board of trustees for the Chickasaw Foundation and is a delegate to the Inter-Tribal Council of the Five Civilized Tribes. He serves the community at large on the board of the Heart of Oklahoma Red Cross

organization. He is a member of Ada Masonic Lodge 119 and is a 32nd degree Mason. He has served with the Army National Guard of Oklahoma as an infantry officer with the 180th Infantry Battalion of the 45th Infantry Brigade, and retired as a captain after 42 years of service. He also serves on the board of directors for the following organizations: Mental Health Services of Southern Oklahoma, Ada City School Foundation, and the Ada Boys and Girls Club.

As an elder and 30-year employee of the Chickasaw Nation, Kennedy Brown is a valuable source of information. He has always been eager to share his knowledge with anyone interested in learning more about this very important time in Chickasaw history. He contributed an oral history to Richard Green's book *Chickasaw Lives: Volume II, Profiles and Oral Histories*, released in June 2009. He also was a valuable source of information for Chickasaw author Phillip Carroll Morgan's book *Chickasaw Renaissance*—a profile of the tribe's twentieth-century experience released in spring 2010.

Currently, Kennedy serves as a Special Assistant to the Governor of the Chickasaw Nation. His duties include listening to and assisting with special needs of Chickasaw citizens. He serves as an ambassador of the tribe to other tribal nations and meets weekly with local and state leaders. He is married to Richenda, and they have one son, Kelly.

Kennedy Brown's philosophy is "to be of service to your fellow man. It is important to listen to people. It is important to be compassionate."

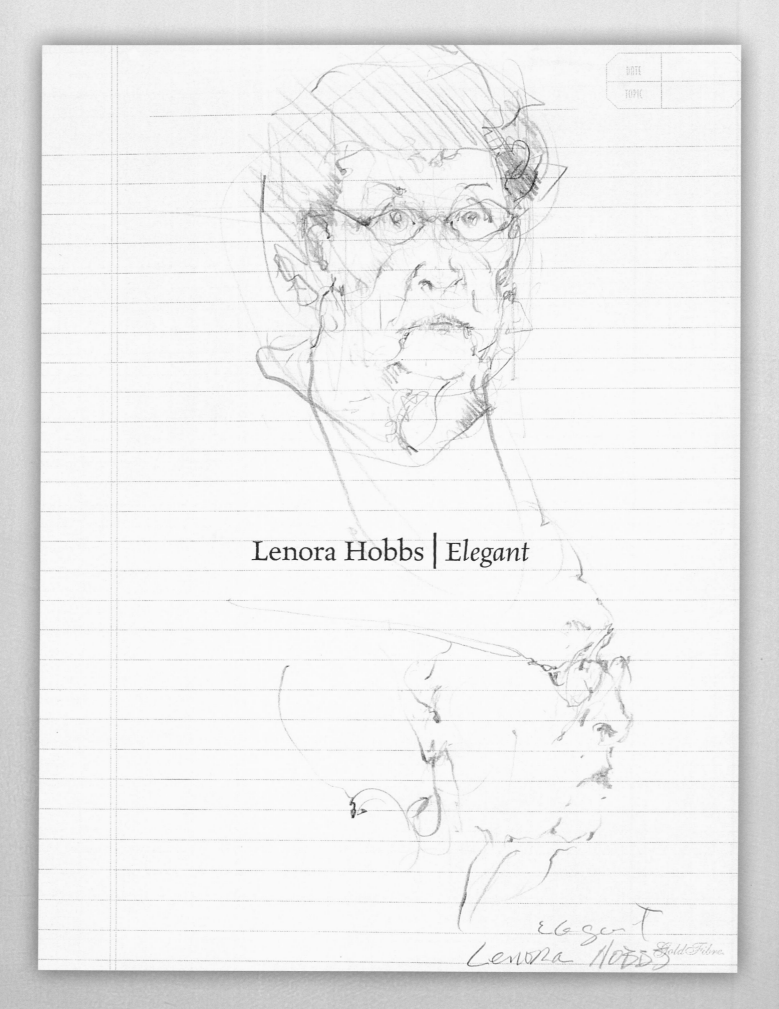

Lenora Hobbs | *Elegant*

Lenora Hobbs was born Lenora Berneice Fuson at Tishomingo, Oklahoma, on September 28, 1915, to Thomas Cornelius and Agnes Fuson. Together the Fusons had ten children, of whom seven were girls, Lenora the eldest. Her family lived on their Chickasaw allotments in a place called Cottonwood. "Our allotments were south of what is now Murray State College. It is all covered in water now. They made it a lake," Lenora notes, sadly.

Thomas Fuson was a farmer. He also worked in a garage and sold cars during the Great Depression. At home, the Fusons raised cattle, chickens, and pigs. "What you raised is what you ate," Lenora explains. "We used to dry fruit, too. We'd have to peel them and slice them. We'd put a sheet on the house or somewhere. We'd use a shed, spread the sheet out and lay that fruit on it in the sun. At night we'd roll it up. The next day we would lay it out again. That's how we kept food. We canned a lot."

Lenora's maternal grandparents were David and Rosa Fulsom. David spoke fluent Chickasaw. "My grandfather spoke, and he would talk to my grandmother. But they didn't teach their children to speak—even my mother. They were afraid it would interfere. They (the children) had to go to public schools. He was originally from Sugarloaf Mountain near Poteau, Oklahoma. My grandfather was full-blood Choctaw. Back in those days, if you were full-blood, you had to have a guardian. He didn't want a white-man guardian spending his money. So he lied a little. He was quite active with the Chickasaws in Tishomingo, especially in building the courthouse (also known as the Chickasaw Capitol Building). I remember when I was a little girl, my aunt had a house just up the street from there, and we would walk across in front of that courthouse. They had an old log cabin; they kept their prisoners in there. They (the prisoners) would yell at us. Scared us to death," remembers Lenora.

The Fuson children went to school in Tishomingo. "I was the oldest one of the ten children, so I helped raise the younger ones. We worked a lot when I was young. I worked in the field chopping cotton," Lenora recounts. They had time to play, too. She and her siblings climbed trees, made toy wheels, and built stilts from tin cans or wood. "We had a Model T Ford, and someone gave my brothers a little goat. That little goat climbed up on that car. It really messed that car up. My brothers also got a little red wagon—a new one. They saved their money for that wagon. They hitched that goat up to the little wagon and that goat ran out the gate and just tore the wagon up," she remembers with a laugh.

After high school graduation, Lenora attended Murray State College. She sang well, so she decided to study music there, and went on to sing soprano in the school's choir, and to perform solo. Following college, Lenora went to work at a variety store in Tishomingo, where she met University of Oklahoma graduate and bookkeeper Lyman Hobbs. After their wedding, the couple moved to Purcell, Oklahoma, where Lyman found a job as an accountant and parts manager for the local Chevrolet dealership in the 1940s. From there Lenora and Lyman moved to Wewoka, Oklahoma, and opened a variety store of their own. "It was kind of a drug store and variety store combined. There was a lot of competition. Then my husband had a heart attack. So we sold that, and came back to Purcell in 1961," Lenora remembered. She got a job at the McClain County Bank. By then Lenora had two sons, Lyman Jr. and John. She also adopted her two younger sisters after her mother died. "I've been here (Purcell) ever since. I've been here in this place for forty-nine years. When we first came here, this was all wilderness."

Lyman Hobbs passed away in 1992, and Lenora still lives in Purcell. After retirement from the McClain County Bank, she stayed active by taking up golf. She also creates ceramic art, dances and goes bowling. Lenora is active at the Chickasaw Senior Site in Purcell.

Lorena Wooley | *Chilocco*

Lorena Wooley was one of six siblings who grew up in a Chickasaw farming family. She was born December 16, 1921, three miles north of Lebanon, Oklahoma. "We were poor. I lost my father when I was about nine and a half years old, in a train and truck collision up close to Oklahoma City," Lorena says, describing the most traumatic time in her life. Lorena's mother was left on her own to rear all six children in Depression-era Oklahoma. "We were poor, but we had a tight-knit family. We created our own entertainment." Lorena remembers swinging on grapevines and getting watermelons to eat during warm, happy days at the creek near her childhood home.

Lorena's family worked hard on the farm. "We had assignments. My oldest sisters made up the beds and swept the house out. My mother went out to milk the cows. I washed dishes, and my eldest brother fed the stock and got everything ready to go to the field." Lorena's resourceful mother used whatever she could find nearby to make whatever the family might need, especially medicines. There were very few doctors around to treat illness in the community where Lorena lived. "She doctored us pretty well," Lorena remembers.

Lorena was sent to Bloomfield Academy in 1927. Bloomfield, established in 1852, provided formal education to Chickasaw girls for many years. "I was in Wiley Hall. It was the dormitory with all the little ones. I was in the baby room. We had three square meals a day. I learned to eat a lot of things that I had never heard of—like pineapple. Pineapple made me sick." Lorena recalls the matrons were very strict. "I didn't like it there." She left while in the seventh grade.

She next attended public school in Madill, and by 1937, was enrolled at Chilocco Indian School. Chilocco, which opened its doors in 1884, taught agricultural trades to American Indian youth, including horseshoeing, blacksmithing, building, printing, shoe repair, tailoring, leatherwork, plumbing, electrical work, welding, auto mechanics, farming, food services and office work. Lorena thoroughly enjoyed her years at Chilocco. "There were murals painted on the walls in the dining room by famous Indian artist Acee Blue Eagle. We had lawn socials where the boys and girls got to talk to each other."

Lorena learned to budget for meals and to cook at Chilocco. Chilocco also taught sewing classes, in which Lorena excelled. She had learned to sew as a small child, and it was something she did well. "I'd already been making my clothes, 'cause we didn't have money to buy clothes. But they (Chilocco) issued everyone a pair of shoes. We called them 'bullhides.' They were just plain black shoes, but you could hardly wear them out. When you polished them, you could just about see yourself in them. Chilocco gave all the girls two or three cotton dresses. They were all made from the same pattern, but with different kinds of material. We got a sweater that was probably from World War I. We had raincoats from World War I, too," she remembers.

Lorena worked in the Chilocco kitchen for a while. "We would work six weeks at a time at one place or another at the school to pay for our room and board." The kitchen fed 800 students at a time. "At suppertime on Saturdays, we always had wieners and sauerkraut. We always knew what we were going to eat on Saturdays." Each spring and fall, Chilocco would hold school-wide picnics. Lorena remembers working with other girls to make large amounts of potato chips for the picnics. She graduated from Chilocco in 1942.

Today, Lorena Wooley lives in Dallas County, Texas. Although her health has suffered over the past few years, she stays active

in the local home extension club, using her sewing talent to help people who might otherwise not get fine things to wear or keep warm by. "I joined the club in 1991. We do volunteer work. We make lap robes for the nursing homes. We've made things for the veteran's hospital. We have also made things for ladies with cancer. And then we made for the 'preemies' (premature babies) down at Parkland Hospital for about two years. It is worse than making doll clothes." Although she has lived a long and full life, the Chickasaw elder still remembers her years at Chilocco as being the best. "I loved every day I went to school at Chilocco!"

Luther John | *Keeper of History*

Luther John was born February 26, 1944, on the grounds of Sandy Creek Presbyterian Church near Fillmore, Oklahoma. His grandparents, Edward and Phoebe Keel John, reared him and are whom he prefers to call mother and father. "My dad was custodian at the elementary school in Fillmore for twenty years. My mother was a homemaker. I was taught Chickasaw by my Mom. She didn't speak very much English at all," Luther recalls. Edward and other members of the family spoke English well, making the family mostly bilingual.

Luther remembers playing in the woods while very young, while his siblings were off at school. "We lived in an area where there was a lot of trees and creeks and things. I would run around in the woods and have no fear. But today, you couldn't get me out there," he cautions, good-naturedly. "I always knew when to get back home, 'cause I knew when lunch was ready. I knew when dinner was ready. I could always time it just about right."

And friends were close, in more ways than one. "Jerry Imotichey lived across the street from us." Luther and Jerry were best friends growing up, and Luther claims to have taught

Jerry and his siblings the Chickasaw language during play times. "It was all Chickasaw, too," Luther insists. "That is where I got both sides, the English and the Chickasaw."

That balance shifted after Luther began school at Fillmore. "When I started school, we used to walk to school. To me, that was the longest walk, and it was only half a mile. We were told not to speak Chickasaw when we first started school. Probably forty percent of the kids were Indian at Fillmore. I remember one Chickasaw family in particular. None of the kids could speak English. They got in trouble a lot. I got in trouble for speaking Chickasaw to them. We were threatened to never speak it again. The government was not the only place that gave Chickasaw students a hard time about language," he recalls.

When summer came, Luther, like other young Chickasaws around Fillmore, went into the cotton fields. "We worked in the cotton fields to get our money for school clothes. When we weren't there, we would go to a swimming hole called Eleven Foot. It was north of where we lived—about a mile on Sandy Creek. It had real pretty rocks all around it," Luther remembers.

After grade school, he attended and graduated from Milburn High School—Fillmore didn't have a high school.

Luther's family lived across the street from Sandy Creek Church, and attended faithfully. "They [church members] would come up on horses, and it was all day. I remember after lunch the men would sit on a log under an old hickory tree on one side and the women would be over here, and it was all Chickasaw. Everything that was told, laughed, kidding—it was all Chickasaw. All of the kids that were at the church had the chance really to learn Chickasaw, because when we were scolded or straightened out, it was in Chickasaw, too. That's pretty much the only time people got to see each other and visit, because they lived too far apart," Luther recalls. "Choctaw hymns were sung at most of the services, and we had wood stoves and kerosene lanterns. Sunday school was taught in Chickasaw, and then later on it just slowly went to English. While the adults were having their meetings, the kids would go swimming in Eleven Foot, or sometimes we would go to Blue River or play ball. It was a lot of fun when I was growing up."

Sometimes, mystery disturbed life near Sandy Creek. Luther's mother once told him about an unusual occurrence. "My mother told me a story about something that happened before my time. She was coming back from Luffy Chapel and she thought she saw the Northern Lights. Before they got to Sandy Creek, it just started lighting up. She said everyone wondered what was going on because it just turned daylight. Even the chickens were out feeding when she got home. They thought it was daylight," Luther explains.

As an adult, Luther traveled to different places across the country. "I worked in L.A. (Los Angeles) for Pacific Bell, and I transferred here to Oklahoma City to Southwestern Bell. I used to climb telephone poles when I was with the Bell Telephone system. After that, I wanted to drive trucks—eighteen-wheelers. I wanted to walk the high iron, and I did that, also. I went to Chicago and I trained at a high-rise building school. I helped build power plants, and I got to walk the high iron. After I did those things, I felt like, 'Well, I can do it'—you know. Then I came back home with my family. I worked at one thing and another, including Sundown Trailers, as a welder, for quite a few years. From there I came to the Chickasaw Nation."

Today, Luther John is retired. He and his wife Judy have lived in the Tishomingo, Oklahoma, area for thirteen years. He has eight children and ten grandchildren, and enjoys singing gospel and speaking Chickasaw. He has taught others to speak Chickasaw through training programs and activities. And, he says, "I love music. As a matter of fact, I've got a little room with my bass, guitar, piano and keyboard.

"The most important thing, however, is my language. I feel like we can make it strong again. We, as Chickasaws, can't let the language go. I am very proud to be Chickasaw. It is what makes us different from other people."

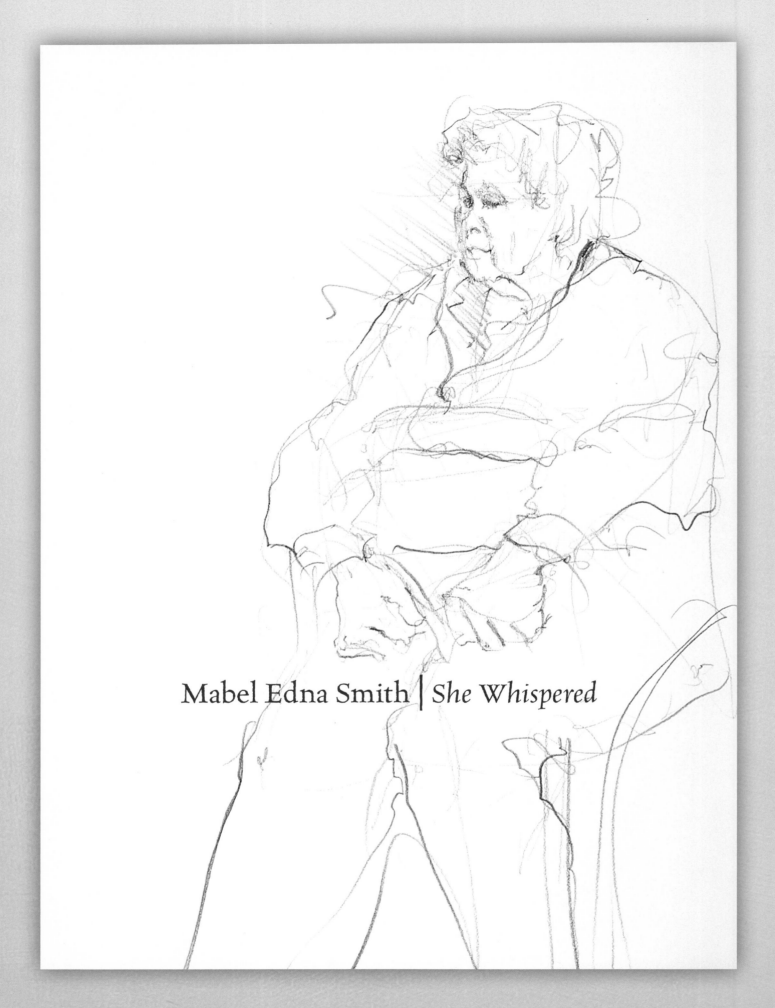

Mabel Edna Smith | *She Whispered*

Mabel Edna Smith was born March 1, 1924, in Lark, Oklahoma, to Cecil Robert and Ellen Ward Laxson. Mabel was a quiet child who enjoyed playing in the woods near home with her younger brothers Jack, Lealon, Eugene and Lonnie.

Her mother was half Chickasaw and spoke the language, however, "My mother regretted never teaching me the language," Mabel recalled. "She always spoke Chickasaw to my grandparents. She said, 'I wished I had taught you how to speak.'" Mabel's grandparents were Houston Ward, a full-blood Chickasaw and Frances Ward, a non-Indian, highly educated and a schoolteacher.

Mabel's mother was a welder during World War II and later worked as a hotel maid. Cecil took a variety of jobs, including oilfield and factory work, to provide for the family. Eventually, Cecil and Ellen separated and divorced, and the Smith children went to live with Cecil in Los Angeles.

Mabel's parents were committed to education for their daughter, so she later was sent back to Oklahoma to board at Carter Seminary.

"My parents and grandparents believed that a good education was important. This way, the white man couldn't take advantage of Indians," Mabel asserted.

She remembered girls of all ages attended the boarding school—and the older girls did most of the work. "When I was at Carter, I worked in the bakery that made their bread," Mabel recalled. "I was also in the choir. One time, WKY radio station in Oklahoma City invited choirs from different cultures to come sing on their program. We traveled on the school bus, and we sang for thirty minutes."

At sixteen, Mabel left Carter Seminary to marry Raymond Smith, who was nineteen. It was the early 1940s, and the young couple struggled financially while the U.S. economy was still trying to recover from the Great Depression. They moved to Phoenix, Arizona, to be near Raymond's parents, Oscar and Maude.

The Smith family did what they could to make ends meet. Raymond and his father and mother worked at a car wash for a time, then for an icehouse, delivering large blocks of ice to business and residences by horse-drawn wagon.

Later, Mabel and Raymond moved to Bakersfield, California, and in time would have six children—Edith, Stanley, James, Victoria, Larry and Leslie. Eventually, Raymond opened a cooling service business. Although they were never wealthy, the Smiths lived a comfortable life. Raymond, like Mabel, felt it was important for his children to get a good education. As a young person, he was not afforded an opportunity to go far in school, and necessity had dictated that he go to work at a very young age—mainly in the cotton fields.

Mabel was a homemaker. She loved her children and delighted in making bread for them—a skill she learned during her boarding school days. She also raised a garden and enjoyed canning produce. Mabel's daughter, Edith Murdock, remembers that well.

"She did this every year. I'd get so aggravated as a child because Mom and Grandma wouldn't let us eat any fruit off the trees. They would say, 'We're going to can that!' We would have to sneak around to eat apricots or plums from the trees. In the fall we would go to Arvin, a little town a few miles away, where the farmers were growing crops. We would come home with a couple of tote bags full of corn. I remember a lot of times sitting there with mom shucking that corn and cutting the ends off so we could can it and put it up."

Mabel enjoyed going to ball games to watch her grandchildren compete, and she made short trips to Las Vegas. "Mom loved pulling those handles at the casinos," Edith recalls. "She really liked to gamble. When people asked, she would always say,

'Well, we made our yearly deposit.' We never won. But we had a great time."

The soft-spoken matriarch—who, like all the ladies in her family, wanted to be called "Granny" in her elder years—made food a major part of Smith family activities and special events. Pashofa and potato salad were mainstays.

"Her potato salad won ribbons at the fair," Edith notes. "There are only five ingredients in it—potatoes, onions, dill pickles, mayonnaise and, eggs. Oh, my gosh, it was so good. Everyone would try to make it—but it didn't taste like Granny's."

Sadly, Mabel passed away March 20, 2008. She left behind many children, grandchildren and great-grandchildren.

"My mother was so proud of the fact that she was Chickasaw," Edith emphasizes. "She always wanted to be able to help her kids. She knew, because of her Chickasaw heritage, her children and grandchildren would be able to get scholarship money to go to school. Education had always been so important to her and my father. It was a wonderful legacy to leave behind."

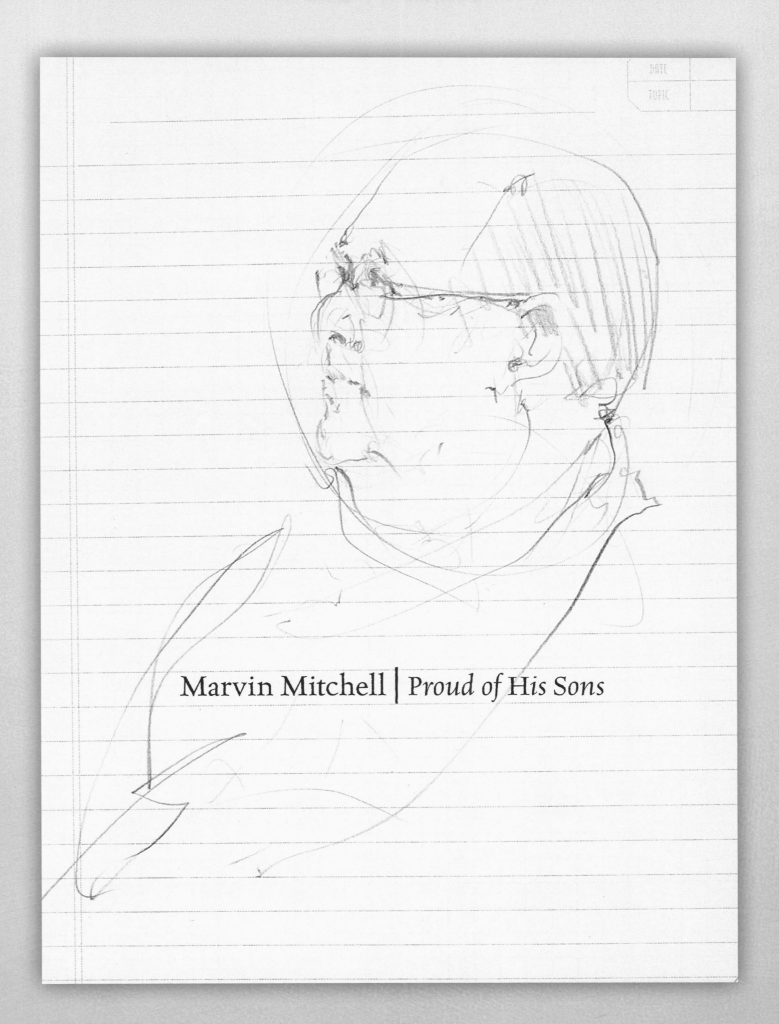

Marvin Mitchell | *Proud of His Sons*

Marvin Ellis Mitchell was born in 1946 to loving parents Ed and Lucile Keel Mitchell. He was the middle child, between older brother Sanders and younger brother Guy. Ed was non-Indian and a sharecropper; Lucile was Chickasaw and a homemaker. The family moved to Jack Fork Creek, Oklahoma, when Marvin was a year old. Later they moved to land near Fitzhugh, and built their home.

"We grew up as Indian kids. My mother had friends among a lot of Indian families. We were just farm kids—growing up like everyone else did," Marvin recalls.

Marvin's grandparents on his mother's side were Sanders and Belle Keel. Sanders spoke the Chickasaw language, and served as an interpreter for the courts in Oklahoma. His experiences led him to warn Lucile about speaking Chickasaw. Marvin gives the reason: "People would have to get up in court and explain themselves. They would be saying one thing and officials would think they were saying something else, because of the language barrier."

The Keels sent Lucile to Bloomfield Academy when she was five years old. By the time she graduated, the school's name had changed to Carter Seminary. She attended Murray State College and Southeastern Oklahoma State University, as well. "My mother could hold her own because she was smarter than everybody else. She was very educated and a refined person in arts and humanities, and social skills. She wanted us to be that way. She was the anchor of our family," Marvin says.

Marvin went to public school at McLish, where a high percentage of Indian students attended. "I participated in Boys Club, basketball and baseball," Marvin recalls. "I was in the Boys Club Hall of Fame. My mother knew Overton James. He was in the state office for Indian education at the time. We went to Oklahoma City to meet with him. He knew of a program for Indian students to go to college. We applied and I got in the program. I was provided tuition and books. I attended college for four years and graduated from East Central State College. I was fortunate."

Marvin grew up listening to his family's stories of shared experiences and ancestors. "My mother used to talk about my great-great-grandfather, Edmund Pickens and his wife (Euthlike Pickens). They came here on the Trail of Tears. I had an aunt that had a mattress that came over on the Trail of Tears.

She made pillows out of it for all of us. All of the nieces and nephews got a pillow out of that mattress. I still have that. It probably doesn't mean a lot to anybody else. But it means a lot to me," Marvin asserts.

The Mitchells worked hard and took pride in their independence. Following his family's work ethic, Marvin took a job as an administrative officer for the Employment Standards Administration. Later he became a federal investigator for the U.S. Department of Labor. He was employed there for thirty-three years. Marvin also served in the National Guard as a master sergeant.

Marvin and his wife, Donna Kaye, had two sons, Mike and Jay Mitchell.

"Mike is the oldest. He is the executive vice president of operations for Chickasaw Nation Industries, Inc., in Norman, Oklahoma. It's a federal corporation outside of the tribe. Jay is an IT manager for the tribal enterprises. They are both military. Mike has been in the Guard for nineteen years. He is a major. Jay has served for eighteen years. He is a chief warrant officer. They both were in Iraq—in fact, they were there at the same time.

They are both recipients of the Bronze Star. I am very proud of my sons—not just for being in the military. I am proud of other things they have accomplished, too. They are both great fathers and good husbands. They have been very successful in their personal lives," Marvin says with pride.

Marvin was a founding member of Chickasaw Nation Industries and serves on its board of directors. He is an elder at the Fittstown Church of Christ, where he has attended many years. "I was raised up Chickasaw all my life. I think of the struggles and the history of the tribe—the proud heritage," Marvin declares. "The best part of being a Chickasaw is being able to give back to the tribe. I feel very privileged. Like my mother, I take pride in being Chickasaw."

Philip Agnew | *Sober Indian*

Philip Charles Agnew lives a very simple life. His closest friends have told him that even at 72 years of age, he has never really grown up. He would say, "No, I just have a passion for living."

That passion began on September 11, 1938, in Austin, Texas, when Philip was born to Edwin Joe and Florence Phoebe Watkins Agnew. "When my dad went to war during World War II, my mother moved back to Tishomingo. She was more comfortable being back where she was born—in Oklahoma, in Chickasaw land," Philip says.

Edwin immigrated to the United States from Ireland and made his living in insurance. Florence was Chickasaw and a homemaker. Together, they raised three children—all sons. The family moved a great deal during Philip's childhood.

"We lived in Oklahoma for a while until the war was over. Then we moved to New Jersey, then Amarillo, and Lubbock. We moved quite a bit when I was small," Philip recounts. "I remember life seemed a lot simpler. My mother taught me to be very proud of my Chickasaw heritage. She was proud of hers. I remember when growing up, sometimes I'd be challenged by something. My mother would talk about my heritage and how it was for me to honor that heritage by doing the best I could—to never give up."

Florence remembered much about her childhood, and shared her memories with Philip through stories. "My mom's mother was Georgia Watkins Jarrett. Mom's father was Eugene Watkins. He was an alcoholic and left the family when my mother was two or three years old. My grandmother remarried and became a rancher in Texas. She became a strong rancher woman herself. My Mom told me a story about when she was two years old. She was playing around a fireplace; there was a fire burning. Her sister threw some bullets into the fire from a gun (pistol) that was hanging on a rack. One of the bullets fired out and hit my mother. Seeing what had happened, my grandmother Georgia hitched up the buckboard and took her to the hospital where a doctor saved her life. She also told me stories about Mississippi and Removal—those that were told by her grandparents," Philip says.

Philip's parents never found the opportunity for much education. "My mom and dad never really finished the eighth or ninth grade. My mom had gone to boarding school for a while. She kept a scrapbook. She could illustrate and write poetry. On one of the pages, she had the newspaper clipping of Sitting Bull's death. She had a beautiful way of writing—her penmanship was self-taught," Philip remembers.

Philip's educational experience began in a one-room schoolhouse in Tishomingo. From there, he attended junior high in Amarillo, graduated from high school in Lubbock, Texas, and went on to study at Texas A&M University. Philip says proudly, "That was a great experience for my family and me. I graduated in 1952." He was the first member of his family to attend college and graduate.

Philip served in the U.S. Coast Guard. He had worked hard throughout his adult life and became a successful businessman until his career was suddenly derailed. "When I was forty, I was president of a large company in Dallas. My bonus in 1980 was a Porsche Carrera. The next year, the board of directors asked for

my resignation. The chairman said it was because of my alcohol problem," Philip admits. "I went all the way down to almost living in a vacant building."

Philip spent the next ten years reconnecting with sobriety. "I met some Native American friends and we became dedicated to fighting the last great enemy of the Indian people—drugs and alcohol," Philip relates. "My commitment is to Native American recovery. When you learn to forgive the unforgivable, then you are on the road to not having resentments. You cease to hang on to the kinds of things that can destroy you."

Philip was married for a time, and had two sons, Philip Charles Jr. and John Morgan. He has one granddaughter, Josephine Corrine.

He later took ownership of a ski lodge near Durango, Colorado, and consulted for the ski industry in Park City, Utah, before the 2002 Winter Olympics. Both his sons became accomplished skiers. During this time, however, Philip was presented with disturbing news.

"I was given a diagnosis by a doctor that was not good. I asked how much time I had left. He said, 'Two to five years.' I said, 'Okay.'

"There were things that I always wanted to do," Philip explains. "I had always wanted to go helicopter skiing in Canada. I got my two sons together, and we did that. I wanted to go kayaking inside passages off of Vancouver Island. We did that. And, I wanted to buy a Harley Davidson. I'd never ridden a motorcycle before. I wanted to ride around America. I told my boys, 'Come get everything I own—all my personal things.' They took what they wanted and I gave the rest to a lady at a secondhand store in Durango. I said, 'Sell the rest of this stuff and give the money to the homeless.' I have six pairs of Wranglers, eight shirts, a good pair of Tony Lama boots and a pair of tennis shoes for walking. I have simplified my life."

Today Philip is retired and lives in Montana. He remains active in programs fighting alcohol and substance abuse among American Indians in his area.

"My Chickasaw heritage has allowed me to be the unconquered— the unconquerable," he says. "My mother instilled that in me when I was young—to overcome the really hard things. She taught me to see things with my heart, not with my mind. It's my spiritual walk; my Chickasaw walk."

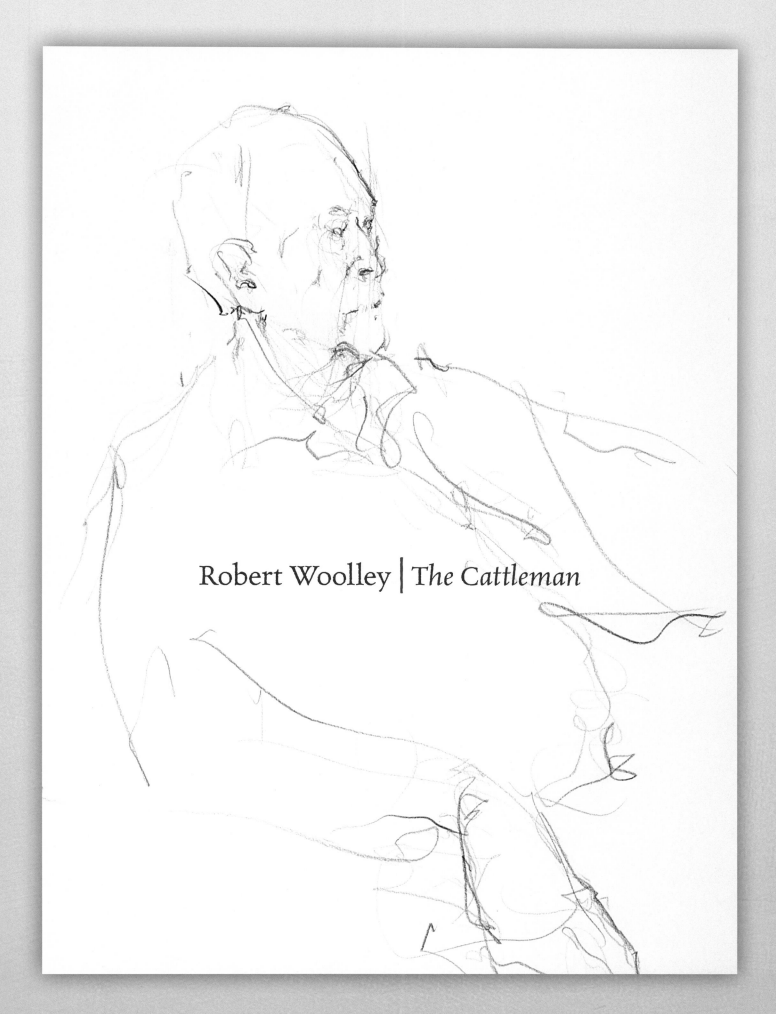

Robert Woolley │ *The Cattleman*

Robert Donnell Woolley was born January 18, 1931, to William Walter and Lillian Burris Woolley, the youngest of their four children after Caroline, William Walter, Jr., and Cecilia. The Woolleys lived in Frisco, Indian Territory (now Stonewall), farming and raising cattle.

Colbert Ashalatubby Burris, Robert's maternal grandfather, was an important figure in Chickasaw history, and a source of family pride. "Colbert came over on the Trail of Tears from Tupelo, Mississippi, when he was about thirteen years old with his mother, sister and a cow," Robert recounts. "He grew up to be a farmer and rancher. After his first wife died, Colbert married Laura Ann Bradley and became active in the early government of the Chickasaw Nation. Colbert was elected as a representative in the tribal legislature in 1859. He also served as a Chickasaw delegate to the meeting of the Five Tribes at old North Fork Town, joining the treaty with the Confederate States of America. Later he helped negotiate the Treaty of 1866. He was also on the Chickasaw Supreme Court for a time. He was an ordained minister of the Methodist church and had a total of seven children. Only two of them survived." At the time of statehood, the Burris family was given allotment lands that eventually became part of a large ranching operation.

The Woolley family, like most in Oklahoma, struggled during the Great Depression. "I was born right after the Great Depression started. During that time, no one could sell cotton. My family survived on what food we could raise. There was no money," Robert explains. "We were mostly farmers—cotton, corn, chickens, pigs and gardens. … I was raised on poke salad."

The Woolley family lived in a modest home. "It was just a frame house. It had one big bedroom that we all slept in. There was a living room, one stove and no running water. I really felt my middle name was 'kindling,' because I was always being told to go get the kindling," Robert recalls with a grin.

Then oil and gas were found on the family's allotment, and improvements followed. "The first natural gas well built in East Fitts Field was drilled right in front of our house. They didn't have any way of controlling it—1,200 to 1,400 feet. It blew the top off the cone and burned up. They finally put it out, but we couldn't light anything for a time," Robert says. "After it was capped, it produced gas for a long time."

Stonewall became a boomtown overnight. "That was the wildest place," he recounts. "Oh, golly, there were beer joints, a filling station, two grocery stores, dance halls, oil field supply house and many other businesses. It was one of the roughest towns you ever saw on a Saturday night. When I was just a kid, I would ride horseback into town. I would sit back and watch people have fights. Oilfield workers came from all over. I might have been ten at the time." As family finances improved, Robert's parents began to travel. "They took me to Alaska," Robert remembers. "We have movies of it. They also went to Cuba and Mexico."

Robert's mother Laura Ann taught him the Chickasaw language. "They (teachers) wouldn't let us use it in school. I went to school with a bunch of Chickasaw children. If we talked Chickasaw, we got in trouble, so we didn't do that. But mother taught me some Chickasaw words like 'shookola'— that's sugar," Robert recalls.

"My first year of school was spent at Stonewall. I went there until my last two years, when my parents sent me to a private school named Todd's Seminary for Boys." It was an independent school founded in 1847 in Woodstock, Illinois, by the Reverend Richard K. Todd, based on principles of "plain living and high thinking in harmony with Puritan traditions." After graduation, Robert attended Oklahoma State University, pursuing a degree in agriculture.

He graduated in 1950, the same year North Korea invaded South Korea, and the United States was about to join the conflict. "I was in ROTC, so I didn't get drafted. But I got my commission there. Since I had graduated, I was expected to go to Fort Benning, Georgia, to officer's training and combat thereafter. I was trained by the 101st Airborne. I graduated from infantry officer school in October 1954," said Robert. He was sent to Fort Riley, Kansas, instead of Korea, and stayed until he retired. "I guess the good Lord was takin' care of me."

Robert went back to the family ranch. "I worked at the ranch till 1959. Then I came to Ada and got into the feed business." Robert later sold the business and took charge of landscaping for East Central State University. He also owned an interest in an auto supply store. He married his high school sweetheart, Patricia Jean Harrell. They had four children, but Patricia suffered from a heart condition that took her life in 1978. Later he married Gwen Carol.

Today, Robert lives a quiet life in retirement. "I was raised in the country—cowboying all my life. I don't have cattle now. I still have my land. It was put in what the family called Woolley Investments—a limited partnership," Robert says. He is a 32nd degree Mason and a member of the Indian Temple. He is a former Chickasaw legislator and served as the Legislature's chairman for several years. He also has served with the Chickasaw Housing Authority. Robert has eight grandchildren and five great-grandchildren. The Oklahoma Historical Society and the Oklahoma Department of Agriculture have honored Woolley Ranch with a designation as an Oklahoma Centennial Ranch.

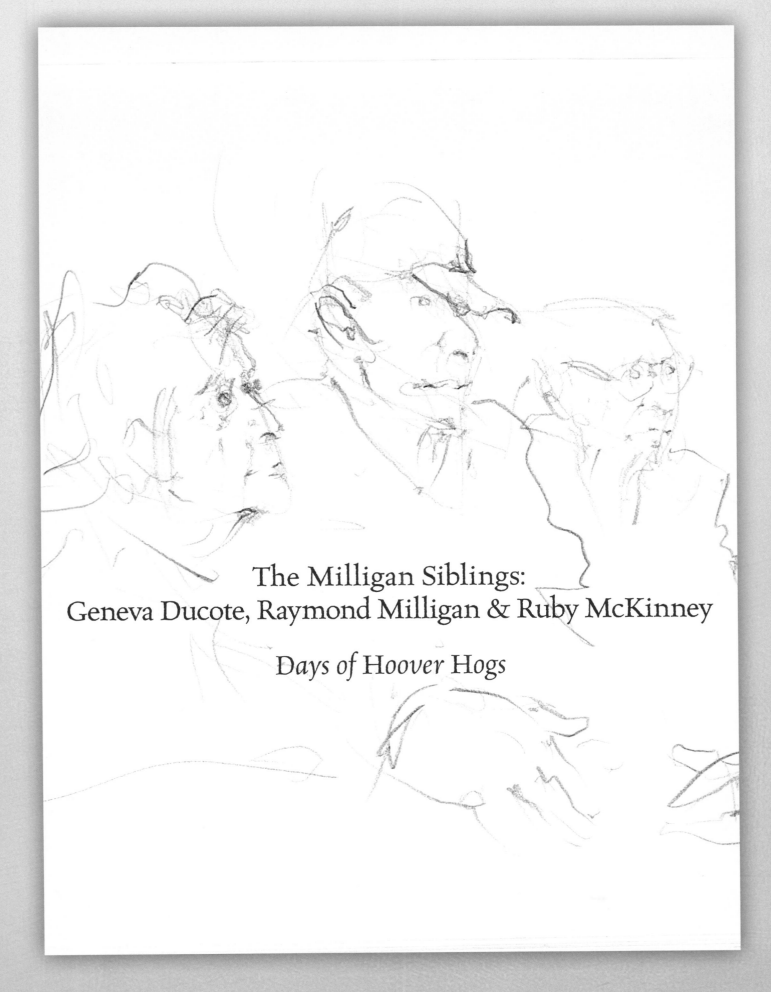

The Milligan Siblings:
Geneva Ducote, Raymond Milligan & Ruby McKinney

Days of Hoover Hogs

Altogether, eight children were born to Richmond Dillard and Caroline Illetewahke Hawkins Milligan—among them Geneva, born May 12, 1929; Raymond, born July 20, 1921; and Ruby, born July 28, 1916.

The Milligans lived on allotment land in Ahloso near Ada, Oklahoma. Richmond was of half-Irish and half-English descent, and seventeen years older than Caroline. He was a carpenter, and helped raise prominent buildings in the Ada area, including the Pontotoc County Courthouse and the First Presbyterian Church. His children recall him as slow to anger, outspoken in his beliefs, and continuously working.

"I saw my poor, old dad come in … sometimes he would leave out before daylight, going to work, and then about eight or nine o'clock, he would come in carrying a big sack of flour, or something else," Ruby recalls. "I don't remember him ever whuppin' me. But he could sit and talk to you. That would hurt as bad as a whuppin' would.

"When he was older, he had a stroke," she says, sadly. "But he didn't want us to take care of him. He wanted to go into the Odd Fellows Nursing Home in Checotah. He said, 'I don't want to be a burden on my kids.'"

Caroline was full-blood Chickasaw, and a hard worker, too. During the day she worked in a laundry, starching and ironing shirts. At night she cooked in a restaurant. "My mother lived long and overcame many things in her lifetime," Geneva says.

And Caroline was firm about some things. "She refused to go to the hospital," Geneva relates. "One time, she had pneumonia. The doctors didn't want to release her. She told them she wasn't staying. People used to say, 'You go to the hospital, you die.' A lot of Indians did die."

Raymond remembers his mother as a healer. "She knew all the old-time remedies."

Ruby stayed home much of the time. "My dad was a carpenter and gone a lot. Momma kept me home. I would help her and work to raise my brothers and sisters. She had eight. But she lost the first child.

"My mother knew a lot about Ada. She said her family used to go to Ada, and there were no streets or roads. She said the first post office was on Fourth Street and the first grocery store was called Reeds." In 1889, Jeff Reed, a mail carrier, built a log home and established the store midway along his mail route of

Stonewall and Center. In 1891, a post office was built and named after Reed's oldest daughter, Ada.

Ruby also discovered her family's connection to history. "I found a sheet of paper where (Caroline) wrote out things about her dad, Julius Hawkins," she recounts. "He built the first church at High Hill Baptist (near Ahloso) out of logs. He was the first deacon there, and helped start the church. His wife, Betsy, was the first Women's Missionary Union (WMU) worker there."

The entire Hawkins family spoke Chickasaw early on, with Caroline as their teacher. "I was around twelve or thirteen when my grandmother died. After that, my mother didn't talk to us in Chickasaw that much. So it kind of got away from me," Ruby laments.

School was no help in that regard. "We couldn't speak Chickasaw in school," Geneva explains. "They would punish us. Some of the kids that went to school, that was all they knew. Our teachers said that if we spoke Chickasaw, we would never learn English."

All the children went to school at Ahloso and Ada, except Ruby, who stayed home to care for her siblings. Geneva also attended Carter Seminary, Chilocco Indian School and college.

Raymond wanted to go to school at Chilocco, but instead was sent to Goodland Academy near Hugo, Oklahoma. "When I got to Goodland, a big ol' heavy guy came out and said, 'I am in charge of you now.' His idea was to beat kids. All those kids ran around with scars on their backs where he beat them. I made up my mind that if he hit me or my brother, he and I were going to tangle," he recounts.

The siblings have a close, loving relationship, strengthened in part by hard times like the Great Depression. "Raymond went to the CCC camp. I remember him going there and sending home money," Geneva recalls.

Ruby adds, "Back then it was 'Hoover time' (a reference to then-President Herbert Hoover), and it was a hard time. My dad worked and worked, all the time. My mother made a garden, and did a lot of canning to make it through the winter. My dad dug a big cellar and kept potatoes, carrots, onions and other things there. It was hard to get something to eat. My brothers would call rabbits 'Hoover hogs.' They'd get together and say, 'Well, let's go get some Hoover hogs.'"

Once grown and out of school, the Milligan siblings made lives for themselves. Geneva and Ruby married and started families.

Raymond joined the Army and served bravely during World War II with the 10th Armored Division in the Battle of the Bulge, earning the Purple Heart and the Bronze Star. Once out of the service, he married and reared five children.

Geneva, Ruby and Raymond express their pride in being Chickasaw.

Geneva believes Chickasaws are "so much more genuine."

Ruby embraces her Chickasaw heritage. "That's all I ever knew. I was close to my mother and grandmother."

One of Raymond's most precious possessions is his Chickasaw Veterans jacket.

Weldon Fulsom | *How Turtle Got Its Shell*

Weldon was born October 16, 1949, at Valley View Hospital in Ada, Oklahoma, to Roy Lee and Nancy Parnacher Fulsom. Nancy suffered from tuberculosis, a contagious bacterial lung infection that can attack other organs. She succumbed in 1954. Weldon was only five.

Weldon grew up speaking Chickasaw, so he started public school as a stranger to English. Roy had to go to class with Weldon to translate. "When the teacher would ask me a question, I couldn't answer it, 'cause I didn't know what they were talking about. So my dad used to interpret," Weldon recalls. "It took me a long time to learn it." However, he did not learn English at school. "I learned it from my cousin," he explains.

"The first school I went to was over there on Rosedale, called Egypt (near Ada, Oklahoma)," he says. "When that closed down, I went to Happyland. After that closed, I went to Tupelo. Then I came back to Ahloso. The last school I attended was McLish (in Fittstown). I moved around a lot in school."

Roy, a full-blood Chickasaw, also contracted tuberculosis but, unlike Nancy, was cured. Unfortunately, Roy also suffered from diabetes.

Weldon remembers hard times when his father couldn't find odd jobs to support them. "I didn't have toys like the boys of today when I was growing up," he explains. "We stayed out in the country and played out in the woods. I would make myself toys and play with them. I played with marbles and tops, too. I liked to fish, hunt and play ball. The only pets I had were three squirrels that my dad gave me." Weldon would spend long hours among the trees until darkness overtook the day or he heard the howls of coyotes.

Weldon grew up going to church, first at Hickory Hill Free Will Baptist Church, an Indian congregation. The family was there for every observance, event and holiday, often furnished with food prepared by expert family cooks—especially traditional fare, like pashofa and grape dumplings. "I used to pick possum grapes for the dumplings," Weldon remembers.

Christian beliefs kept Roy away from Chickasaw stomp dances. But Weldon remembers his father attended pashofa dances for healing the sick. Roy knew traditional healing practices, and was taught by his father, Charlie Fulsom, about the medicinal elements found in nature. "I learned a few things from my dad,"

Weldon says. "I use cottonwood for any kind of bone splinter—I split it and put it on my arm. I use broom weed for a bad cold. You boil it and drink it."

Roy and Weldon lived with an uncle until 1975, when the first Indian homes were built in the Chickasaw Nation. "We didn't know a home was going to be built for us until they (tribal officials) came and told us. At first, my dad didn't want it. They asked him to sign a piece of paper. They took the paper and built it," recalls Weldon. Soon after, Weldon and his father moved in, and Weldon cared for Roy there until his death in the spring of 1993.

Weldon's first job, at sixteen, was in a janitorial position at McLish schools. Later, he worked twelve years for J.T. McConnell Septic. He then was hired at the Chickasaw Nation, and has been a tribal employee since. "I am a van driver for the senior citizens. Now that they have the buses, I don't drive as much as I used to. I like working with the seniors best of all. They are good people," Weldon says. He also helps at the Ada Senior Citizen Site, cleaning and loading supplies.

Today, Weldon lives in Ada with his wife Robin in the same Indian home built for him and Roy in 1975.

Weldon remembers some of the traditional Chickasaw stories he learned from his father. One is about how Turtle got his shell:

"You know how the top of a turtle shell looks like a puzzle? Well, it wasn't like that in the beginning. Mother Skunk chopped it up. One day, Mother Skunk went to go hunt some food for her little ones. The little ones were inside a hole, so Turtle went and asked them where their mother was. The baby skunks told him where Mother Skunk went. She had gone to dig some potatoes, and that's what Turtle wanted. He told them, 'When she gets back, you all can have all the big potatoes. Save the little potatoes for me.' He left and Mother Skunk came home. You know how turtles have those red eyes? Well, the baby skunks told their mother a red-eyed man came and wanted to know where Mother Skunk was, and that he wanted all the small potatoes that Mother Skunk brought home. They were to put the small potatoes under the bed. The Mother Skunk knew who he was, so she picked up a hatchet and went after Turtle. When she caught up with him, she chopped him up into pieces, and left him there on the ground. Turtle lay there for a while. Then, he called for the gnats to come eat his fat and other stuff. He also asked them to sew his shell back onto his back. That is why he looks like that."

Zane Browning | *Too Tall*

Zane Browning was born January 26, 1936, three miles north of Mill Creek, Oklahoma, on his grandfather's allotment. He was the youngest of four brothers, each of whom would grow to heights above six and a half feet. His upbringing was rural and quiet, as with many Indian families living nearby. Like other Chickasaw children of his generation, he attended church. "I remember growing up with the church, and attending all-night singings at a little place called Bellwood," Zane says.

After graduating from Mill Creek High School in 1955, Zane traveled to Lawrence, Kansas, to attend Haskell Institute, an industrial school maintained by the government for Indian girls and boys. After college, Zane entered the work force as a cowboy on former Oklahoma Governor Roy Turner's ranch near Sulphur, Oklahoma. Zane remembers, "I went to work up there, $140 a month, room and board, six and a half days a week. We got to sleep late on Sunday morning." While working on Turner's ranch, Zane received a telegram that would set the course of his life. He was granted an interview by the Muskogee Area Office of the Bureau of Indian Affairs (BIA) for a job at the Sequoia Vocational School in Tahlequah.

A year later, Zane was promoted to payroll supervisor, a move that opened the door for him to enter the BIA's management training program. After he completed the program, he was transferred to Gallup, New Mexico, to work among Pueblo tribes and the Navajo. He moved up the career ladder again after he became administrative officer for the Job Corps center in Winslow, Arizona. A year and a half later, Zane took another leap upward at the BIA to a chief payroll supervisor position. Later, he moved to Phoenix to take a job as a loan specialist for the BIA. From there the BIA transferred Zane to Pawnee, Oklahoma, where he worked with the Otoe Missouria, Pawnee, Ponca, and Tonkawa tribes.

It was about this time that the American Indian Movement (AIM) came to public attention. AIM was and remains an Indian activist organization advocating for indigenous American interests. The organization gained worldwide attention when it seized the BIA headquarters in Washington, D.C., in 1972, and the infamous standoff a year later on the Pine Ridge Indian Reservation at Wounded Knee, South Dakota.

"That (Wounded Knee) was a bad deal," says Zane. "We (the BIA) did not like it at all. But I tell you what AIM accomplished. The publicity they got brought attention to the Bureau of Indian Affairs, and forced them to rethink their policies. It was a big change."

Zane moved from Pawnee to Anadarko, and later became the Assistant Area Director of Administration. His next job with the BIA was located at the Muskogee Area Office. He was back where he started—but much farther up the career ladder in the federal government offices. His new position gave him the opportunity to work with the Five Civilized Tribes, including his own people, the Chickasaw.

He later became superintendent at the Ardmore Area Office, which dealt primarily with the Chickasaws. By that time, the Indian Self-Determination Act was in force, and the Chickasaw Nation was rebuilding its government. The tribe had about 20 employees, most serving as Community Health Representatives (CHRs). From 1979 to 1993, Zane helped to establish Chickasaw Nation compacts for control over many BIA programs under the Indian Self-Determination Act. In 1991 he received the Meritorious Service Award from the Department of the Interior in recognition of his dedicated service and outstanding contributions on behalf of Indian people. Zane also served as CEO for the Chickasaw Nation for a year.

He retired from his long service with the Bureau of Indian Affairs in 1993. Zane lives with his wife Judy in Mabank, Texas. Together they have three grown children—Brian, Teri and Cheryl.

Bernard Courtney | *Water Bread and Water Gravy*

Bernard Nelson Courtney was born September 22, 1939, at the Choctaw Hospital in Talihina, Oklahoma, one of twelve children born to William and Mattie Lee Woodcock Courtney.

"There were nine living kids in the family, and I was the only one born in the hospital. A set of twins didn't make it—would have made eleven kids. There was a boy younger than me that didn't make it, either," Bernard says.

Bernard's father, William, was full-blood Chickasaw, born in 1897. "He had quite a life before I came along. Then he became a preacher man. He was Full Gospel," Bernard recalls.

Not only that, William delivered babies, which Bernard thinks may explain his siblings' births outside hospitals. "He used to go around the country and deliver kids here and everywhere—like a doctor. I would go with him sometimes."

William's congregations were a mix of Indians and whites. "He pastored a church over in Wapanucka, Oklahoma," Bernard says. "Then he pastored a church twelve miles south of Madill, at a place called Bethel. After that, he never pastored anymore. He had a cancer that was eating away at his spine; he didn't know he had it. When he was sick, he could hardly walk. When the Spirit hit him, though, he would get happy and jump five feet in the air. He died when I was a teenager in 1956. He was 59 years of age."

Bernard's mother, Mattie, was part Irish, Choctaw and Cherokee, and planted award-winning gardens. "She got a blue ribbon for the best garden one year," Bernard says proudly. "Wherever we lived, we would make gardens. We ate out of the garden a lot."

Bernard remembers his mother kept a spotless home and cooked on a wood stove. In Madill, the family lived in a one-bedroom house, lit with oil lamps at night. Some children slept with William and Mattie, while others, including Bernard, slept on the back porch.

William spoke five languages fluently, one of them Chickasaw. "He would only teach us to speak Chickasaw when we were eating," Bernard recalls.

"There were times when we had nothing more to eat than water bread and water gravy. That is bread made out of just flour and water. The gravy wasn't made with milk. It was made with water and flour, too.

"I was out hunting squirrels at the age of twelve with a gun. We would eat the squirrel head, the eyeballs, the tongue and the brains. We loved them," he says.

Bernard remembers Mattie as a conservative woman who smiled very little and wore her hair in a plaited bun until quite later in life, when "she finally cut her hair—even shortened her sleeves and her dress to her calves. She laughed more," he recalls.

Bernard attended school until the seventh grade. "By this time, I was with my older sister in Arkansas. I stayed with her and went to school in Mulberry, Arkansas, for a couple of weeks. For some reason or other, I got in trouble with the principal. One day he pulled me and another guy up in front of everybody, and took a leather strap and wore us out. I never knew what it was that we had done. I quit school right there," Bernard says.

Bernard had a variety of jobs. "When I was a kid, I did quite a bit of hoeing. When I was twelve years old, I completed my first master cylinder job on a Chevy. I took it out, overhauled it, and put it back in by myself. I had no one to tell me if I was doing it right or wrong. After that, I was in the cotton patch, pulling

cotton for a little bit of money. I worked in the hay fields. Then I went into cutting up old cars and taking the iron off of them. I got where I could pick up a whole half a car by myself and throw it on a truck at the age of sixteen."

In 1960 Bernard married Janet Kay Wheeler. He was twenty-one years old; she was sixteen and living in Enid, Oklahoma. Together they would have three children. "At one point, we decided to go to Bozeman, Montana, and I started working as a dishwasher for a dollar and a penny an hour. We rented an apartment that was furnished and bills paid for thirty-five dollars a month. I also worked in a dry cleaner. I have about fifteen years experience as a truck driver. I spent a few years as professional welder—and I followed the powwow circuit and made pretty good money crafting leather goods and repairing broken silver. I also danced there," Bernard recounts.

Eventually, Bernard and Janet would move to Oklahoma City, where he operated a 90-ton crane, worked on gin trucks and loaded pipe at oilrig sites. Later, the couple moved to Florida, where Bernard went to work for the Miccosukee Indian Village near Ochopee. He and Janet will have their fiftieth wedding anniversary in November 2010. They have seven grandchildren, four great-grandchildren and four great-great grandchildren.

"In my lifetime, I've had so many different experiences and different jobs. You'd be surprised," said Bernard. "My dad used to say that he did so many different things that he should be 300 years old. The same happened to me."

Mike & Martha Larsen

Mike Larsen, Artist

Mike Larsen was born in Dallas, Texas, to a Chickasaw father and Caucasian mother. He spent his younger years between Wynnewood, Oklahoma, and Amarillo, Texas. Mike's father was not active in his life, so his mother, maternal grandparents, and later his stepfather saw to the shaping of his life and character.

He knew in college that he wanted to be a fine artist. Even the teacher who told him to find another line of work because he had no talent could not douse his drive. Beginning at Amarillo Junior College, continuing at the University of Houston, and concluding at the prestigious Arts Students League in New York City, Mike studied traditional art disciplines.

For forty years Mike has been a full-time artist. Over the past twenty years, galleries throughout the United States have represented him. While still represented by galleries of note, Mike now spends most of his time painting and sculpting privately commissioned work. The summer of 2010 saw his largest commission unveiled at the St. Joseph Regional Healthcare System in Paterson, New Jersey. It is a twice-life-size sculpture with four figures representing the health care givers and those they attend.

Mike's love for painting and sculpting dancing figures began when he was commissioned by the State of Oklahoma to paint a twenty-six-foot-long mural for the Capitol Rotunda of five internationally prominent ballet dancers, all born in the state. He has been honored to paint several series of murals for institutions throughout the state of Oklahoma, which all portray the history of the state he calls home. Added to this honor was being chosen by the United States Postal Service to create the Oklahoma Centennial Stamp.

With his love of American history, Mike will achieve a personal goal in 2011, researching and painting murals for the Oklahoma History Center on the Civil War in Oklahoma. The Battle of Honey Springs was an important part of history in the West, and important to the efforts of the Confederacy to win the war in Oklahoma.

One of the highlights of Mike's career has been to paint the living elders of the Chickasaw Nation. His second series of paintings is presented in this book. Because of the great acceptance of the people he painted, and those who helped facilitate the project, Mike has become a true family member of the Chickasaw Nation.

Martha Larsen, Writer

Martha Larsen was born in 1953, the fifth of six children, and grew up in Hutchinson, Kansas, and Enid, Oklahoma, where her father worked as a pump line operator for Champlin Petroleum. Being raised in a Catholic family by parents who survived the Great Depression left an indelible mark on Martha. She and her siblings learned at an early age to be self-reliant and industrious, and retasked clothing (then known as "hand-me-downs") was the fashion for the family.

Martha attended Oklahoma State University. She had a good eye for design, which led her to establish a small picture framing business, where she eventually met the artist Mike Larsen, and the rest, as they say, is history.

Now the business side of Larsen Studio & Gallery, Martha also began assisting Mike in many studio undertakings early in their marriage, including photography of various subjects. During the research for the Chickasaw Living Elders Project, she has been the photographer of all the subjects during their interviews. "Our life in art would not be nearly as successful without our joint efforts as a team," says Mike.

In addition to creating and maintaining their Web page, Martha finds time for artistic endeavors apart from her famous husband's work: gardening, knitting, carpentry, and overseeing the building of their home and Mike's studio.

After living in Oklahoma City while their children were attending and graduating from the Putnam City schools, Mike and Martha realized their dream of building a home on a nice piece of land in a much smaller town. Having become involved in the community, Martha is a past member of the Perkins Community Foundation and the Centennial Plaza Trust. She is currently the Chairman of the St. Francis Xavier Catholic Church Parish Council and is active in the church community.

Mike Larsen
Curriculum Vitae

www.larsenstudio.com
P.O. Box 160
Perkins, OK 74059
405-210-4945
mike@larsenstudio.com

Education
1984 Art Students League, New York, NY
1968 University of Houston, Houston, TX
1964 Amarillo Junior College, Amarillo, TX

Major Public and Private Commissions
2010 *Proud to Be Chickasaw* published by the Chickasaw Press, October
2009 Opening of the exhibit I *am Very Proud to be Chickasaw*, Gaylord-Pickens Oklahoma Heritage Museum, November, Oklahoma City
2009 Oklahoma Book Award Finalist (*They Know Who They Are*)
2009 Commissioned by the Oklahoma History Center to create murals and paintings in commemoration of the sesquicentennial of the American Civil War in Oklahoma
2009 Commissioned by St. Joseph's Regional Medical Center, Patterson, New Jersey, to create a monumental-size bronze for a newly constructed entrance
2008 *They Know Who They Are* published by the Chickasaw Press, October
2007 Opening of the exhibit *They Know Who They Are*, Oklahoma History Center, November 2, Oklahoma City
2007 Commissioned by the Pokagan Band of the Potawatomi Tribe to create eight historical murals
2007 Oklahoma State Centennial Postage Stamp goes on sale
2007 Two monumental size bronzes unveiled at the Oklahoma City Civic Center, which were commissioned by the Oklahoma Centennial Committee
2006 Commissioned by the Chickasaw Nation to create a second series of paintings of Living Elders
2006 Named 2006 "Oklahoman of the Year" by the state magazine, *Oklahoma Today*
2006 Unveiling of the Oklahoma Centennial Postage Stamp
2006 Commissioned by the Oklahoma State Centennial Committee to create two monumental size bronzes to represent the arts
2005 Commissioned by the United States Post Office to create the stamp for the Oklahoma Centennial to be issued in 2007

2005 Commissioned by the Chickasaw Nation to create 24 paintings of Living Elders

2004 The painting *Battle of the Washita* is chosen as the cover image for *Washita – the U.S. Army and the Southern Cheyennes, 1867 – 1869* by Jerome A. Greene

2004 Six murals commissioned by The University of Oklahoma for The Reynolds Performing Arts Center and the University of Oklahoma School of Dance

2003 Commissioned by National Bank of Commerce for the first in a series of "Oklahoma Artists"

2002 *Council at Oak Tree*, painting depicting the historic Creek Council tree in what is now Tulsa, OK; Oklahoma State Capitol

2001 *The Young Dancer*, commissioned for the Oklahoma City Art Museum

2000 Eight Murals at Quartz Mountain Lodge, Oklahoma Institute of Art, Lone Wolf, OK—four document Kiowa history and four document the disciplines of art taught at the institute

1995 *Cloud People*, Federal Reserve Bank of Kansas City, Oklahoma City, OK branch

1993 Six paintings commissioned by Turner Publishing used to illustrate *The Native Americans: an Illustrated History*, a six-part television documentary and book (see bibliography)

1991 *Flight of Spirit*, (22 ft. by 11 ft.) mural, Great Rotunda, Oklahoma State Capitol, Oklahoma City, OK. Five Native American Ballerinas: Yvonne Chouteau, Rosella Hightower, Maria Tallchief, Marjorie Tallchief, and Moscelyne Larkin.

Awards

2000 Inducted into the Chickasaw Nation Hall of Fame

1997 "Spirit of Oklahoma Award," Master Show, Five Civilized Tribes Museum

1995 Named "Master Artist," Five Civilized Tribes Museum

1994 Best of Show, American Indian and Cowboy Artists

1992 First Place in Oil Painting, Santa Fe Indian Market

1989 First Place in Drawing and Second Place in Painting, Red Earth Festival

1988 First Place in Drawing and Second Place in Painting, Red Earth Festival

1988 First Place in Oils, Colorado Indian Market

1987 Grand Award, Red Earth Festival (the first Grand Award given)

1984 First Place in Sculpture, Trail of Tears Museum, Tahlequah, OK

Selected Bibliography

2009 *Art Focus Oklahoma*, "Painter of History," November/December

2009 *The Daily Oklahoman, I am Very Proud to be Chickasaw* exhibit review, December 23

2008 *Western Art Collector*, "Fleeting Moments of Intensity," January

2008 *Home and Away* (AAA magazine), "The Art, The Murals, The Majesty," July/August

2008 *Distinctly Oklahoma*, "He Conquers Who Endures," September

2007 *Persimmon Hill*, magazine of the National Cowboy and Western Heritage Museum, January

2007 *Mistletoe Leaves*, magazine of the Oklahoma Historical Society, January

2007 *The Journal of Chickasaw History and Culture*, "The Three Stages of Mike Larsen"

2007 *Oklahoma Today Magazine*, January/February

2006 *The Daily Oklahoman*, December 30

2006 *Oklahoma Today Magazine*, November/December

2005 *Art of the West*, June/July

2004 *The Perkins Journal*, May 6

2003 *Art Treasures of the Oklahoma State Capitol*, Oklahoma Centennial Project

2003 *American Indian*, magazine of the National Museum of the American Indian, cover, Winter

2001 *Sunday Oklahoman*, "Old Meets New at Quartz Mountain Showplace," April 1

2001 *Nichols Hills News*, "Keeper of the Flame," January

2000 *Cowboys & Indians*, July

2000 *Oklahoma Today*, "City Folk," July/August

2000 *Oklahoma Today*, "Sacred Ground," May/June

1998 *Cowboys and Indians*, "A Gathering of the Ancient Ones," February

1998 *Art of the West*, "Double the Talent, Double the Fun," January/February

1998 *Southwest Art*, "Shamans of the Nations," May

1998 *Phoenix Home & Garden*, March

1996 *Art Talk*, cover and story, February

1996 *The Sunday Oklahoman*, photo of painting on front page and story, March 3

1996 *Oklahoma Today*, "Good Medicine," cover and story, June/July

1996 *Artscene*, "Exploring Other Dimensions with Symbolic Art," January/February

1995 *The Nashville Network*, feature story

1995 *Southern Living*, October

1994 *People*, "The Native Americans," October 10

1994 *Tulsa World*, "Capitol Full of State Treasures," January 21

1993 *The Native Americans: An Illustrated History*, Turner Publishing, Atlanta, GA

1993 *Southwest Profile*, "The Ancient Ones," February/March/April

1993 *Art Talk Magazine*, "Mike Larsen," June/July

1993 *Mike Larsen, Profile of an Artist*, Video by Little Deer Productions

1992 *Dance Magazine*, June

1991 *Southwest Art*, "Mike Larsen," cover and story, June

1991 CNN, feature story on *Flight of Spirit*

1991 *Art of the West*, "Native American Warrior Featured in Pentagon Exhibit," March/April

1991 *New York Times*, "Chronicle-Salute to Dancers Brings Them Together Again," November 18, 1991

1990 *Oklahoma Today*, "Dreams and Visions: Travelers on a Common Ground," cover and story, November/December

1989 *Art of the West Magazine*, "I Am a Seeker," March/April